PUB STROLLS IN
NOTTINGHAMSHIRE

Peter Fooks

COUNTRYSIDE BOOKS

NEWBURY BERKSHIRE

COUNTRYSIDE BOOKS
3 Catherine Road
Newbury, Berkshire

To view our complete range of books,
please visit us at
www.countrysidebooks.co.uk

ISBN 1 85306 677 X

Photographs by the author
Maps by the author and redrawn by Techniset Typesetters
Designed by Graham Whiteman

Typeset by Techniset Typesetters, Newton-le-Willows
Produced through MRM Associates Ltd., Reading
Printed in Singapore

Contents

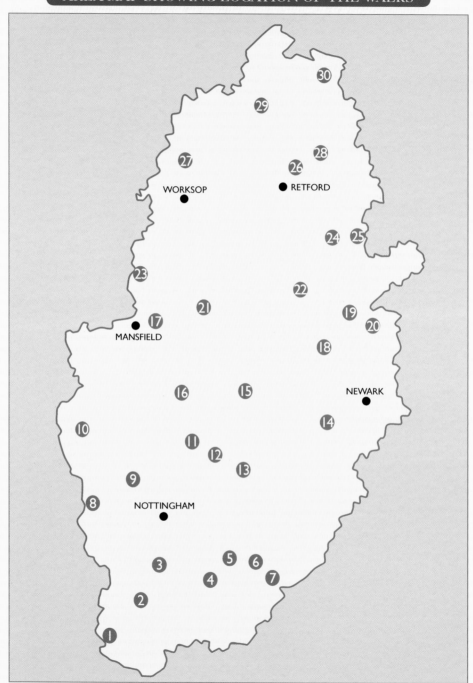

PUBLISHER'S NOTE

We hope that you obtain considerable enjoyment from this book; great care has been taken in its preparation. However, changes of landlord and actual closures are sadly not uncommon. Likewise, although at the time of publication all routes followed public rights of way or permitted paths, diversion orders can be made and permissions withdrawn.

We cannot, of course, be held responsible for such diversion orders and any inaccuracies in the text which result from these or any other changes to the routes nor any damage which might result from walkers trespassing on private property. We are anxious though that all details covering the walks and the pubs are kept up to date and would therefore welcome information from readers which would be relevant to future editions.

The sketch maps accompanying each walk are not always to scale and are intended to guide you to the starting point and give a simple but accurate idea of the route to be taken. For those who like the benefit of detailed maps, we recommend that you arm yourself with the relevant Ordnance Survey map in the Explorer series.

From the point of view of the average regular walker, Nottinghamshire is one of the less favoured areas. We have no mountains, and no seriously demanding moorland. We have no National Parks, no designated Areas of Outstanding Natural Beauty and very few National Trust properties. It should not be assumed, however, that there is nothing here to appeal to the wayfarer. This is the county of Robin Hood, the poet Lord Byron, the novelist D. H. Lawrence. And we have Sherwood Forest, the Dukeries, the Vale of Belvoir and the South Notts Wolds, each with a beauty of its own.

Our country pubs will bear comparison with any others. Many of them date back several centuries, still maintaining their old-style atmosphere, but without the spit and sawdust. All of them have been sampled by the author (over a period!) and are guaranteed to provide excellent food, drink and service. Most of the proprietors will allow you, if you are visiting the pub, to leave your vehicle in their car park while you complete the stroll. But do not take consent for granted – common courtesy demands that you ask first. It is also a good idea, if your footwear is muddied in the course of your walk, to remove it before entering the pub.

Those not intending to visit the pubs should not, of course, use the pub car parks. Where alternative public facilities exist, these are mentioned in the preliminary details of the walk. If no such facilities are available, non-users of the pubs should park considerately in a suitable roadside space.

Not everybody, of course has his or her own transport. All of the strolls are understood to be accessible by some sort of bus service. But services inevitably vary both in frequency and reliability. Your nearest bus station should be able to provide information or try the Buses Hotline (telephone: 0115 924 00 00 or 01777 710550).

A walker's best friends are his or her feet so some sort of sound, strong footwear is important. The absolute minimum, I would suggest, is a pair of good quality trainers with suitable cleated soles.

As with the pubs, all of the strolls have been physically checked out prior to inclusion. All are less than 4 miles in length, which should place them well within the capacity of most moderately fit individuals. Being 'Strolls', they are expected to appeal to the occasional ambler rather than the seasoned rambler. But if any more hardy individuals wish, once in a while, to tackle something a little less demanding – please be my guest! One or two of the strolls, as indicated in the details, are considered to be manageable, wholly or in part, by accompanied wheelchair users and baby buggies. Bearing in mind, of course, that some of the way may be over uneven ground.

If you have not yet sampled the joys of strolling our Nottinghamshire footpaths, lanes and byways, give it a try. Take the kids – and the grandparents – and the dog (but keep him on a lead when occasion demands). Walk in the steps of Robin Hood, D. H. Lawrence and Henry Kirke White. I guarantee you will be agreeably surprised!

Peter Fooks

Sutton Bonington
The King's Head

MAP: OS EXPLORERS 245 and 246 (GR 505251)

WALK 1

DISTANCE: $2\frac{1}{2}$ or $3\frac{3}{4}$ MILES

DIRECTIONS TO START: FROM THE A60 AT REMPSTONE, FOLLOW THE A6006 WEST FOR $4\frac{1}{2}$ MILES, TURNING RIGHT INTO PARK LANE AFTER CROSSING THE RAILWAY BRIDGE, AND CONTINUING FOR A FURTHER MILE. THE KING'S HEAD IS ON THE LEFT. **PARKING:** AT THE KING'S HEAD (PATRONS ONLY) OR TIDILY, ON-STREET.

The village of Sutton Bonington started life as two separate hamlets, known, not surprisingly, as Sutton and Bonington. A pleasant and attractive place with a comfortable mixture of ancient buildings and more recent structures, the village extends for a little over a mile along a single main road, with the railway forming a distinct barrier on the east. This was, in former times, a centre of the framework knitting industry with, in the middle of the 19th century, as many as 50 workshops making stockings.

Agriculture, the other staple industry hereabout, still flourishes; as it should, of course, since the University of Nottingham's College of Agriculture is located here in Sutton Bonington.

For much of the way, this most delightful stroll follows the banks of the Soar, Nottinghamshire's most beautiful river (which we share with Leicestershire). There is generally plenty of wildlife to be seen, as well as a steady flow of river-craft and narrow boats, particularly at the weekend.

The King's Head

Rumour has it that former patrons of the King's Head include the one-time Official Hangman, Mr Pierrepoint. Also that the inn has its own resident ghost. I am assured that there is no known connection between the two. This is a Union Pub Company house, providing both Marston's and Mansfield ales. The atmosphere is warm and friendly, and the ambience clean and homely, with discreet brass, copper and chinaware adorning the tastefully decorated and furnished lounge bar. Food is restricted to excellent filled cobs and sandwiches. There is a children's play area and outside drinking area.

Midday opening is from 12 noon until 3 pm on Sunday to Friday, extended to 4 pm on Saturday. Evenings from 6.30 pm to 11 pm on Monday to Friday, 7 pm to 11 pm on Saturday and 7 pm to 10.30 pm on Sunday. Telephone: 01509 672331.

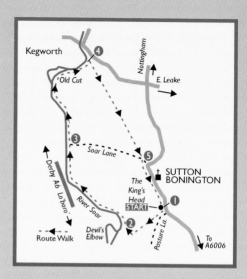

The Walk

① Leaving the pub, turn right, then right again into Pasture Lane. Past the last of the houses, the lane narrows. Cross a stile on the right (by a guidepost) and follow a faint path down the centre of the field for its full length. Cross a farm bridge and stile, turning right in the next field to follow the hedge. Cross the low concrete flood wall to join the riverside path, and turn right.

② Follow the riverside path, resisting the urge to swim over to an enticing pub (the Otter) on the opposite bank. Pass the marina and continue to the junction with Soar Lane. Those souls wishing to shorten the route may do so by following Soar Lane back to Sutton Bonington.

③ For the full route continue ahead, still following the Soar. A short length of canal,

The 'Old Cut'

The River Soar

the 'Old Cut', bypasses a dangerous weir. This ends at the Kegworth Deep Lock, after which the path continues over an open field.

④ Where the river bends left, and close to an electricity pylon, turn sharp right over the field, leaving the riverside and following a faint track. The path becomes clearer in the next field, as it continues over a series of arable fields and pastures, passing through a thicket to reach a private access lane. Cross the lane and continue straight ahead over the fields (Sutton Bonington's church spire your guidemark) to reach Soar Lane.

⑤ Go straight forward to Main Street, and continue back to the King's Head.

PLACES OF INTEREST NEARBY

Donington Grand Prix Collection, to the south-west of Castle Donington. Situated just off junction 23a of the M1 and adjoining the Donington Park racing circuit, the world's largest collection of single-seater racing cars is on display to the public. Open daily throughout the year, from 10 am to 5 pm (Christmas opening subject to confirmation). Telephone: 01332 811027.

Gotham
The Cuckoo Bush

MAP: OS EXPLORER 260 (GR 536302) **WALK 2** **DISTANCE:** $2^3/_4$ MILES

DIRECTIONS TO START: TURN SOUTHWARDS OFF THE A453 SOUTH OF NOTTINGHAM AT THE ROUNDABOUT BY THE CRUSADER PUB IN CLIFTON AND FOLLOW THE UNCLASSIFIED ROAD VIA CLIFTON PASTURES TO GOTHAM. THE CUCKOO BUSH IS ON THE RIGHT, IMMEDIATELY BEFORE THE CHURCH. **PARKING:** AT THE CUCKOO BUSH INN; BUT A RECOMMENDED ALTERNATIVE IS THE PUBLIC PARKING AREA ADJACENT TO THE CHURCH.

The people of Gotham have long endured a reputation for foolishness. In fact, the Gothamites are not, and never were, so stupid as the legends suggested. For the story behind the tradition tells of a very canny body of villagers who, to avoid the predicted expense and upset of having a royal hunting lodge wished upon them, contrived to convince the King's emissaries that they were all a few cards short of a full deck. The fact that the King got the message, and decided to put his lodge elsewhere, goes to show that the villagers were right in their contention that 'more fools pass through Gotham than remain in it'.

We are not all, perhaps, completely foolish, but some of us are obliged to pass through Gotham. The wiser ones will remain here for long enough to sample this delightful stroll via the track of the old mineral (gypsum) railway and along the ridge of Gotham Hill.

The Cuckoo Bush

A Punch Taverns house, the name of this attractive and traditional village pub commemorates the most famous exploit of the 'Wise Men of Gotham', who built a fence round a bush to keep the cuckoo in, 'so that he would sing to them all through the year'. Cheerful and snug, with the date of foundation (1858) over the door, the interior decor incorporates a delightful clutter of china, brass and bric-a-brac. Families are welcome; so are well-mannered dogs.

Meals and bar snacks are provided from 12 noon until 2 pm daily, also on Thursday and Friday evenings, and an excellent range of delicacies is supplemented by the familiar daily specials board. The opening hours from Monday to Friday are 12 noon to 2.30 pm and 5 pm to 11 pm. All day opening on Saturday and Sunday. Telephone: 0115 983 0306.

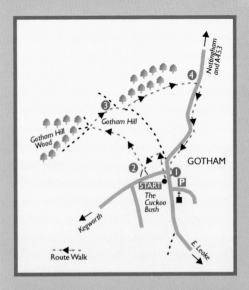

The Walk

① Follow Leake Road past the Kegworth Road junction, continuing along Nottingham Road as far as the bend. Keep straight on here, leaving the road in favour of the rough track alongside the British Legion Clubhouse. Turn left through a picnic area, following the footpath along the old mineral railway, now designated as the 'Gotham Railway Walk'.

② After following the railway walk for some way, leave it via a footpath on the right, immediately beyond a park bench. Continue along the field path, on the left of the hedge, ascending gently towards the wooded hills. Passing through a kissing gate, bear left with the cart track. Pause at the next stile to enjoy the rearward view before continuing over the hilltop field. Pause again on the highest ground, where superb distant views extend in every direction. Ignore a gate leading into Gotham Hill Wood,

The Gotham Railway Walk

11

On Gotham Hill

turning right here, and passing another gate, on your left. Continue along the field boundary over Gotham Hill.

③ Through a metal bridle gate, cross over to the edge of the wood and turn right, following the edge of the wood. Keep to the side of the wood over uneven ground, and pass through a bridle gate. Continue by a clear track over fields, descending to join a redundant section of the Nottingham road by a riding stables. (Round about this spot, one of the Wise Men is alleged to have stopped on his way to Nottingham market, and sent his cheeses on ahead. The cheeses, not being fully trained, ended up in the ditch!)

④ Turn right, joining the vehicular road, and continue back to Gotham village.

PLACES OF INTEREST NEARBY

Manor Farm Animal Centre and Donkey Sanctuary, Castle Hill, East Leake. Open Sundays and bank holidays from 10 am until 5 pm (4 pm in winter). Friendly animals, straw maze, indoor and outdoor activity areas and café. Telephone: 01509 852525.

Clifton
The Crusader

MAP: OS EXPLORER 260 (GR 545344) **WALK 3** **DISTANCE:** 3¼ MILES

DIRECTIONS TO START: APPROACHING FROM NOTTINGHAM, FOLLOW THE A453 AND PASS THE TEACHER TRAINING COLLEGE AND CLIFTON VILLAGE GREEN. THE CRUSADER, WHICH OVERLOOKS THE ROUNDABOUT WHERE THE GOTHAM ROAD LEAVES THE MAIN A453, IS ACCESSED VIA HARTNESS ROAD. **PARKING:** AT THE CRUSADER. IF NOT VISITING THE PUB, THERE IS A PUBLIC CAR PARK ON HOLGATE, PARTWAY ROUND THE WALK.

At the end of the 1939/45 war, Clifton was still a peaceful and pretty village on the quiet lane between Wilford and Gotham. The Hall was still, as it had been for centuries, the home of the Clifton family. The village green was still a place where children danced round the maypole on May Day. Many of the old thatched cottages remained, as did the beautiful and famous grove of mature elm trees. There have been a lot of changes in the interim; not all of them sympathetic to the village's traditional character.

Yet all is not lost. There is still much about Clifton village to please the mind. Starting from the Crusader pub (one of the more welcome changes!) we pass quickly through a small and quiet housing estate to reach open country. We skirt the top end of the village and descend to the banks of the Trent and, after following the riverside path, return through Clifton Grove and village, back to the start.

The Crusader

The Crusader – a Kimberley Ales house – is a clean and smart modern estate pub, in an ideal position to attract the local residential custom, and to catch the passing trade on the busy M1 link road. Meals – and bar snacks – are provided here daily, Monday to Saturday, between 12 noon and 2 pm. The menu incorporates all the popular favourites as well as vegetarian meals, and the range of snacks and light bites includes filled rolls, baguettes, toasties and hot snacks. Families are welcome (sorry – no dogs) and there is a special children's menu for the small people. Parties are catered for – subject to prior booking.

The pub is open all day, every day; from 11 am to 11 pm on Monday to Saturday and from 12 noon to 10.30 pm on Sundays. Telephone: 0115 984 4534.

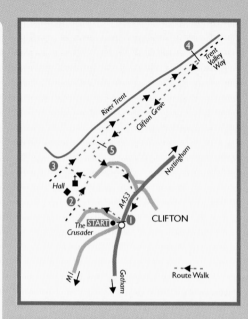

The Walk

Note: This route should be manageable by wheelchair, subject to coping with a large metal 'step-over' beside the Holgate car park.

① Follow Hartness Road away from the roundabout, turning right on reaching Hawksley Gardens to reach a farm lane.

② Turn right, follow the track past Home Farm and continuing along Yew Tree Lane. Turn left at the road junction. Go left again, following Holgate. By the entrance to the public car park (opposite the hall), branch right beside a metal barrier gate, descending a steep rough track to reach the riverside.

③ Turn right by the guidepost, following the riverside bridleway. This is a fine, firm path, well suited to wheelchairs and baby buggies; and well wooded, adding to its charm.

④ After following the riverside for about a mile – and just before reaching a guidepost – turn sharp right, doubling back along a narrower path and ascending the hill to reach Clifton Grove. This path doubles as the River Trent Greenway, and

PLACES OF INTEREST NEARBY

Ruddington Framework Knitters' Museum, Chapel Street, Ruddington. Award winning working museum, showing the life and labour of a Victorian knitting community. Demonstrations, video presentations and shop. Telephone: 0115 984 6914.

Clifton green and dovecote

a section of the Trent Valley Way. A broad green way, and formerly, we suppose, a driveway to Clifton Hall, the Grove has long been a popular spot with succeeding generations of Nottingham folk, and was immortalised in verse by Henry Kirke White – and, in *Sons and Lovers*, by D. H. Lawrence. The famous avenue of elm trees, which fell victim to the dreaded Dutch Elm disease, was duly replaced with chestnuts. These are now coming to full maturity. And are no doubt popular, in the conker season, with all the wee lads of Clifton! Continue for the best part of a mile.

⑤ Leave the Grove at last via an enclosed footpath (guideposted) on the left. Join the road, keeping straight forward down Groveside Crescent. Turn left at the village street. Keep to the right as you pass the green, turning right at the A453 road and following the pathway back to the Crusader.

Normanton on the Wolds
The Plough

DIRECTIONS TO START: NORMANTON LIES JUST OFF THE A606 SOUTH OF NOTTINGHAM. APPROACHING FROM THE CITY, FOLLOW THE A606 AND GO THROUGH EDWALTON. ABOUT 2 MILES AFTER THE LINGS BAR ROUNDABOUT, PASS THE JUNCTION FOR COTGRAVE (TRAFFIC LIGHTS) AND TAKE THE NEXT TURNING ON THE LEFT (OLD MELTON ROAD). THE PLOUGH IS AT THE FAR END OF THE VILLAGE. **PARKING:** LIMITED PARKING IS AVAILABLE AT THE PLOUGH, BUT THERE SHOULD ALSO BE AMPLE ROADSIDE SPACE AVAILABLE OPPOSITE THE PUB.

Normanton on the Wolds – one of a number of Nottinghamshire Normantons – is little more than a hamlet; a dormitory suburb of Nottingham and, until the bypass intervened, a junior partner of the rather more significant village of Plumtree. That bypass has been the salvation of Normanton, having left the village in blessed seclusion astride the unspoilt Old Melton Road, undisturbed by the infernal combustion engine. The Wolds of the title are the gently rolling wooded hills of the South Notts/Leicestershire border, the suffix being attached to a number of villages in this area.

This short and easy stroll takes us over pleasant fields with wide views across the Wolds and Cotgrave Forest and, beyond the local landmark of Hoe Hill, to the city of Nottingham. We return via the quiet rural lane from Clipston on the Wolds, and a small modern housing estate.

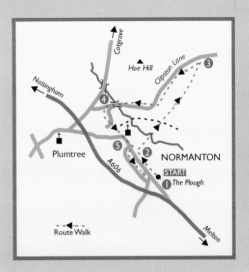

The Plough

A Pub Estates Company house, 'Normanton's Bestkept Secret' is a lovely traditional old village pub with ivy-covered exterior walls, and ancient beams, pewter mugs, horse brasses and copperware brightening the interior décor. There is a warm and convivial atmosphere, two cosy bars and a large attractive garden area. Families are welcome, but the licensing conditions mean that children under eight are only allowed in the dining areas if accompanied by an adult, and while having a meal. Dogs are allowed in the garden area (and, in the evenings, in the bar areas), but must be kept on a lead. Bar snacks (including superb ham cobs) are available at lunchtimes only, but full meals can be had at lunchtime and in the evening, with separate menus for each period, as well as the usual daily specials board.

Opening hours are from 11.30 am to 3 pm and 6.30 pm to 11 pm on Monday to Thursday, 12 noon to 4 pm and 7 pm to 10.30 pm on Sunday and all day (11 am to 11 pm) on Friday and Saturday. Telephone: 0115 937 2401.

The Walk

① Follow Old Melton Road back through the village.

② Turn right over a stile, at a footpath sign, initially following a broad enclosed track. Continue ahead over the fields, crossing Polser Brook and ascending easily,

with Hoe Hill prominent on the left. Cross a farm access road, carrying on ahead along a well-used footpath, keeping to the highest ground and enjoying excellent wide views, over to Nottingham on the left and the South Notts Wolds to the right.

③ Turn left at the road (Clipston Lane),

Normanton

Back Lane, Normanton

following this peaceful country lane gently downhill.

④ After recrossing Polser Brook, take the first turning on the left (The Leys), a small estate of modern houses. Keep to the pavement on the left, looking out for an enclosed footpath – which you will find beside no 6, a metalled pathway between tall Cupressus hedges. Turn right after crossing a footbridge and continue into Normanton village.

⑤ Keep straight ahead along Old Melton Road, as far as Heather Cottage. Turn right here into Back Lane, and continue round, back to the Plough.

PLACES OF INTEREST NEARBY

Nottingham Transport Heritage Centre, Mere Way, Ruddington (west of the A60, within Rushcliffe Country Park). A great day out for the family, with fun for all ages. Steam passenger trains and classic bus rides, plus a superb miniature railway. Souvenir shop and cafeteria. Open Sundays and bank holidays from April to October. Telephone: 0115 940 5705.

Cotgrave
The Rose and Crown

MAP: OS EXPLORER 260 (GR 644355)   **WALK 5**   **DISTANCE:** 3¼ MILES

DIRECTIONS TO START: TURN SOUTH-EAST OFF THE A52 AT THE HOLME HOUSE TRAFFIC LIGHTS, THEN TURN RIGHT BY THE SHEPHERD RESTAURANT, CONTINUING TO COTGRAVE. THE ROSE AND CROWN IS ON THE RIGHT, BEFORE THE VILLAGE CENTRE. **PARKING:** AT THE ROSE AND CROWN, FOR PATRONS ONLY. THOSE NOT VISITING THE PUB ARE RECOMMENDED TO USE THE PUBLIC CAR PARK AT COTGRAVE (CANAL) BRIDGE.

The village of Cotgrave has seen a lot of changes in a relatively short space of time. Fifty years or so ago, this was no more significant a place than most other Nottinghamshire villages. Then a seam of coal was found, bringing in an influx of new blood, and a spate of housing. The wheel has turned full circle now. The pit is gone, its site developed as a Country Park. Yet the legacy remains, if only in the Tyneside accents of many of the older residents. Apart from its mining heritage, there is much else of interest in Cotgrave; not least the extensive woodlands of Cotgrave Forest, and the rural beauty of the Grantham Canal. And Cotgrave sired the local framework knitter and poet 'Rusticus' (George Hickling), who lived from 1827 to 1909.

The stroller will encounter and appreciate some of those rare qualities in the course of this little saunter, over the fields and along the banks of the canal.

The Rose and Crown

The Rose and Crown, on Main Road, claims to be the second oldest building in Cotgrave; there are no prizes for guessing which building is older! Belonging to the Whitbread Pub Partnership, the pub's age is not revealed, but its attractive, traditional style, with old beams and bare brickwork within suggests a certain vintage. The exterior is equally attractive, with hanging baskets adding a delightful touch. The place was refurbished in 1998, but still retains the atmosphere of a genuine village inn.

There is all day opening here, from 11 am to 11 pm on Monday to Saturday and 12 noon to 10.30 pm on Sundays. Food is served – meals and bar snacks – daily from 12 noon until 9 pm on Sunday to Thursday and until 10 pm on Friday and Saturday. There is an outside drinking area, and non-smokers are catered for. Telephone: 0115 989 2245.

The Walk

① Follow Main Road into the village. At the road junction by the Manvers Arms, turn sharp right into Church Lane, passing the church, recently seriously damaged by fire, but now completely and beautifully restored. Bear right with the lane, to join the waymarked Tollerton footpath. In the field, the path branches – the less obvious route, to the left, is the one to take. This passes behind the houses to continue along the 'foot' of the L-shaped field, now on the left of the hedge. Through a hand-gate, continue ahead along a wooded path. Emerging

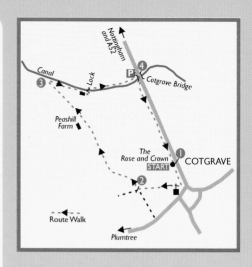

again into a field, turn right and follow the hedgeside to reach a lane, and turn right.

② Pass the sewage works, bearing left with the lane. Where the track bends sharp left at a double set of gates, keep straight forward through a hand-gate (beware the ditch!) now following a field path on the right of the hedge. Continue beside a paddock, crossing a lane to the right of Peashill Farm. Where the hedge terminates, keep straight forward on the same line to reach and cross a stile, turning right onto the canal towpath.

PLACES OF INTEREST NEARBY

National Water Sports Centre, Adbolton Lane, Holme Pierrepont (a couple of miles or so north of Cotgrave) – 270 acres of parkland providing a home for an international 2,000 metre regatta course, white water slalom course and water ski lagoon. A wide range of water activities is suitable for complete novices as well as Olympic grade performers. Plus gentle walks within the Country Park and beside the River Trent. Open all year; admission free. Telephone: 0115 982 1212.

Swans on the Grantham Canal

③ This section of the Grantham Canal is still 'in water' and the adjacent towpath is nicely surfaced, making for pleasant strolling. You will usually see some wildlife here – when I checked out this walk there was a family of swans in residence, consisting of cob and pen and six cygnets, as well as one or two mallard 'swanning around'. Waterhens are also quite common, and the occasional heron is not unknown. From the Lock Keeper's Cottage there is a choice of routes. The former towpath here doubles as an access road, and the preferable option is to cross the restored lock and use the footpath along the opposite bank. Both routes lead back to the Cotgrave Bridge car park.

④ At the car park, turn right and follow the road back to the Rose and Crown.

Cropwell Bishop
The Lime Kiln

MAP: OS EXPLORER 260 (GR 678345)   **WALK 6**   **DISTANCE:** $3\frac{3}{4}$ MILES

DIRECTIONS TO START: THE LIME KILN IS SITUATED ONE MILE EAST OF THE FOSSE WAY (A46), ON THE INTERSECTION OF THE COTGRAVE TO COLSTON BASSETT ROAD WITH THE CROPWELL BISHOP TO KINOULTON ROAD. **PARKING:** AT THE LIME KILN (PATRONS ONLY) OR TIDILY, ON LANESIDE.

Although nominally associated with Cropwell Bishop parish, this walk is wholly outside the main village area, having a closer affinity with the tinier settlement of Owthorpe. This is essentially an agricultural area, on the fringe of the peaceful Vale of Belvoir, but the legacy of industry is still around; in the forlorn, almost forgotten remains of the Grantham Canal, and the still-present evidence of gypsum mining hereabouts. Owthorpe, though – unlike the larger Cropwell Bishop – remains a purely rural community and a haven of peace. But it had its own Manor House, once the home of Colonel John Hutchinson, Parliamentary Governor of Nottingham at the time of the Civil War.

A walk of peaceful, lightly trodden ways follows the quiet towpath of a section of the Grantham Canal, before paying a brief visit to Owthorpe, with its square-built village church and nearby ancient fishponds.

The Lime Kiln

No doubt owing its name to the local gypsum mining and quarrying industries, the Lime Kiln stands on a country crossroads, a good half mile from the village of Cropwell Bishop. There is a nice atmosphere here, with a clean, smart and pleasantly attractive modern décor, tasteful furnishings and smiling service. This is a free house, offering a full and varied menu of steaks, curries, lasagne, omelettes and specials, as well as salads and quick snacks. Not forgetting Sunday lunch. Families are welcome; so are well-behaved dogs, and there is an attractive outside garden area (complete with aviaries) and a children's play area.

Opening hours from Monday to Saturday are between 11.30 am and 3 pm and from 7 pm till 11 pm. Sunday opening is from 12 noon to 3 pm and 7 pm to 10.30 pm. Telephone: 01949 81540.

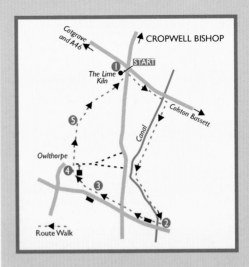

the (roofless) pigeon loft. Continue over the crossroads, following Park Lane towards Owthorpe.

③ Just after a row of cottages, cross a stile on the right, following the waymarked route towards Owthorpe village church. Do not enter the church grounds, but follow the wall round to the left and through a gate.

The Walk

① Follow the lane towards Colston Bassett, turning off right to join the canal towpath. There is little water to be seen in this section of the canal, which has long been out of use and is largely choked up with weeds, reeds and a thriving young tree or two. But it is pleasant walking nonetheless, for about a mile along a nice firm track.

② Turn right at Owthorpe Road (Spencer's Bridge), passing Oddhouse Farm, an attractive building with some interesting-looking outbuildings. Note

The lane past Oddhouse Farm

23

Grantham Canal, near Owthorpe

④ Cross over to the next stile, keeping straight ahead beside a house and on over the field. Cross another stile and continue beside a fishpond.

⑤ Bear left over the next stile, following the hedgeside to the top of the field; then bear half-right over three fields and through a farmyard to reach the road.

Turn left, back to the Lime Kiln.

PLACES OF INTEREST NEARBY

Holme Pierrepont Hall, reached from the A52 at Gamston is an early Tudor manor house in a quiet rural situation, with Pierrepont family portraits and regional furniture. Summer opening only. Telephone: 0115 933 2371.

Colston Bassett
The Martins Arms

MAP: OS EXPLORER 260 (GR 698332)   **WALK 7**   **DISTANCE:** $2\frac{1}{4}$ MILES

DIRECTIONS TO START: FROM HOLME HOUSE TRAFFIC LIGHTS ON THE A52, FOLLOW THE STRAGGLETHORPE ROAD, CROSSING THE A46 (FOSSE WAY). TURN RIGHT AT THE ENTRANCE TO CROPWELL BISHOP AND LEFT AGAIN BY THE LIME KILN, CONTINUING FOR $1\frac{1}{2}$ MILES TO COLSTON BASSETT VILLAGE. TURN RIGHT BY THE VILLAGE CROSS, INTO SCHOOL LANE. **PARKING:** AT THE MARTINS ARMS (PATRONS ONLY) OR TIDILY, SCHOOL LANE.

A most attractive Vale of Belvoir village, Colston Bassett is one of Nottinghamshire's undoubted gems. The relatively modern parish church, with its tall and graceful spire, was built in 1892 by the husband of Alice Catherine Knowles; in her memory, and that of their son who was killed in a drowning accident. The earlier church of St Mary, which it replaced, still stands, a sad ruin of its former glory, on the far side of the Hall Park. The slender village cross is one of only three National Trust properties in the county.

This short and gentle stroll is full of interest. After crossing the little River Smite, the way passes close to the pitiful ruins of the ancient church of St Mary. Then on through the Hall grounds, enjoying a full face view of the Hall itself, before finally recrossing the Smite and passing the cross, back to the pub.

The Martins Arms

The Martins Arms occupies a secluded position on a quiet cul-de-sac, close to the village centre and the ancient National Trust maintained village cross. This popular 300-years-old free house has a fine old Jacobean fireplace and period furnishings, and hunting scenes upon the walls. It has received numerous awards for its food and even the gardens have achieved award status. There is a wide range of real ales on offer, including Marston's Pedigree, Bateman XB and XXXB and Morland Old Speckled Hen. Strongbow cider is available on draught and a distinguished range of whiskies and brandies is provided. Local fare is served daily, including Sunday, from 12 noon until 2 pm; also on Monday to Saturday only between 6 pm and 10 pm. Specialities of the house include Colston Bassett Stilton cheese and Melton Mowbray pies, alongside such exotica as spiced breast of duck with a bramble and shallot compote. Cooking is done to order, using fresh ingredients. Where appropriate, a charcoal grill is used for certain dishes.

Opening hours are from 12 noon until 3 pm throughout the week; and in the evenings, Monday to Saturday from 6 pm until 11 pm and Sunday from 7 pm to 10.30 pm. Families are welcome; and dogs (in the garden area only). Telephone: 01949 81361.

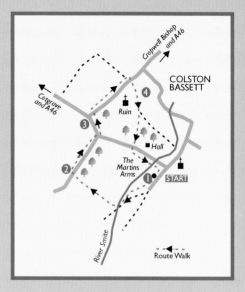

The Walk

① Follow School Lane away from the village. At the end of the houses, cross a stile on the right and follow the waymarked route over the field. Cross the River Smite and continue beside the facing fence – and succeeding hedge. Pass through the gateway, following the green field track to reach Owthorpe Road.

② Turn right, then go left at the road junction. Pass a gatehouse on the right, turning right again at the next junction (New Road), signposted for Cropwell Bishop and Langar

③ Follow New Road – initially with woodland on either side. Beyond the woods, the ruins of St Mary's church come into view ahead and to the right. Continue up the slight hill, with the woodland of Blanche's Gorse on your left. Turn right and follow the rough track

PLACES OF INTEREST NEARBY

Naturescape Wildflower Farm and Visitor Centre, is in Langar (Coach Gap Lane, off Harby Road), just to the north-east of Colston Bishop.

The ruins of the ancient church of St Mary

towards the old church. St Mary's dates back to the 13th and 14th centuries and was, in its time, one of the most beautiful in the county. Sadly, it fell into disrepair with the building, in 1892, of the new village church of St John the Divine. But something of its ancient beauty still remains, despite the necessary barrier of a safety fence. And it is clear that many of the locals still prefer to take their eternal rest upon this quiet hilltop site.

④ The track passes to the left of the church; continue forward towards the cricket field. After passing through a gateway, but before reaching the little pavilion, bear right where the path branches and enter the woodland of the Hall Park. Cross the lawn – it is a public footpath! – and continue to the road. Turn left, recrossing the River Smite and passing the village cross, back to School Lane and the Martins Arms.

Cossall
The Gardeners Inn

MAP: OS EXPLORER 260 (GR 482436)   **WALK 8**   **DISTANCE:** 3 MILES

DIRECTIONS TO START: LEAVE THE A610 (EASTWOOD BYPASS) VIA THE A6096, AS FOR ILKESTON. GO LEFT AT NEXT JUNCTION, PASSING THROUGH AWSWORTH. THE GARDENERS INN IS AT THE FAR END OF AWSWORTH, ON THE LEFT. **PARKING:** AT THE GARDENERS INN (PATRONS ONLY); PUBLIC PARKING SPACE IS ALSO AVAILABLE AT WESTERN END OF NEWTON'S LANE.

A particularly charming and unspoilt village today, it is difficult – despite persistent proposals to resume opencasting nearby – to appreciate that the earliest documentary evidence of coal mining in Nottinghamshire relates to workings in the Cossall area in 1282. This is a very real oasis, as popular with today's generation of countrylovers as it was with the great D. H. Lawrence. Nearly two hundred years ago, three local men went to war, fighting Napoleon's army at Waterloo. Only one came home; the others losing their lives on the battlefield. A monument to all three still stands in the churchyard, alongside a similar memorial to the fallen of more recent conflicts.

This gentle route takes us along a stretch of the Nottingham Canal; no longer navigable here, but still 'in water' and dedicated as an attractive nature reserve. Ascending to the village, with an opportunity to view the Waterloo memorial, we continue via easy field paths and lanes, back to our starting point.

The Gardeners Inn

A Kimberley Ales (Hardys and Hansons) house, the Gardeners is one of our newer locals, a large and comfortable estate pub on the edge of the neighbouring township of Awsworth. Built in 1959, it was refurbished and extended in 1991, and the proprietors are members of 'Cask Marque', a scheme dedicated to excellence in the provision of cask ales. Food is served daily from 12 noon until 2 pm; also, from Monday to Friday, between 6 pm and 8 pm. Families are welcome (dogs too, but only outside) and there is an outside drinking area as well as a children's play area.

Opening hours in the week are from 12 noon to 2.30 pm (3 pm on Saturday) and between 6 pm and 11 pm, with all day opening on Sunday from 12 noon until 10.30 pm. Telephone: 0115 932 3087.

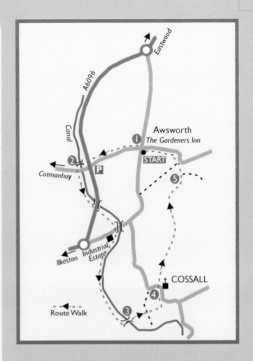

The Walk

① Cross the road and follow Newton's Lane through to its end (cul-de-sac) adjacent to the A6096. Over the main road, join the unclassified (Cotmanhay) road and cross the canal.

② Turn left onto the towpath. The canal has been out of commission for many years and is no longer navigable. The section to the north of the Cotmanhay road is still fished by local anglers (an unusually sociable breed – they all favoured me with a cheerful greeting as I passed by); this part, however, is rather more overgrown – but it still has water and is dedicated as a nature reserve with wildfowl (mainly waterhens) and flora – including yellow toadflax. Not to mention – if the nearby road signs are to be believed – migratory frogs or toads in season. Pass an aqueduct and an industrial estate, continuing ahead, with arable and grass fields on either side.

③ On reaching a crossing turn left, following Mill Lane up the hill.

PLACES OF INTEREST NEARBY

Shipley Country Park, just over the border in Derbyshire, has a Visitor Centre in Slack Lane, Heanor, to the north of Ilkeston. There are woodlands, meadows and lakes, with a network of good paths. Also a shop, a café, cycle hire and toilets. Disabled facilities. Admission free; telephone 01773 719961 for full details, including opening hours.

Nottingham Canal, at Awsworth

Continue to Cossall village and a road junction, and turn left along Church Lane. The Waterloo monument is on the right, just inside the church gates; the more recent memorial on the left.

④ Turn left by the church, and immediately right. This is a private drive – but gives access to the field path, via a stile, a little way along on the left. Over the stile turn right, following the hedgeside down the field and continuing over two further fields. At a four-way guidepost, take the 'Kimberley and Strelley' option, passing through the gap in the hedge and continuing on the right of the hedge, and round to a grass exit lane. The map shows the path as crossing this field diagonally, but all the evidence on the ground points to the perimeter route.

⑤ Join a farm lane and continue ahead, following the metalled lane round the leftward bend and on, back to the Gardeners.

Watnall
The Queen's Head

MAP: OS EXPLORER 260 (GR 501461)   WALK 9   DISTANCE: 3$\frac{1}{4}$ MILES

DIRECTIONS TO START: FROM NOTTINGHAM AND THE M1 (JUNCTION 26), FOLLOW THE B600, TURNING RIGHT BY NUTHALL CHURCH AND CONTINUING FOR ABOUT 1$\frac{1}{2}$ MILES. THE QUEEN'S HEAD IS ON THE RIGHT. **PARKING:** AT THE QUEEN'S HEAD (PATRONS ONLY) OR ON ADJACENT RESIDENTIAL ROADSIDE.

The village of Watnall forms a part of the parish of Greasley, having no church of its own; and no 'Big House' any more, following the death of Sir Lancelot and Lady Maud Rolleston and the subsequent sale and demolition of the Hall at Watnall Chaworth. Apart from two excellent local pubs, few of the older buildings remain. Watnall pit has gone, and an industrial estate now occupies the site of its former railway wharf. So it might be supposed that Watnall is of little relevance today. But that would be an error – for Watnall is the venue, every August, of the ever popular Moorgreen Show, when farmers and country lovers flock here in their thousands.

This route offers easy walking over broad acres, where our farmers still ply their craft – and show their livestock and produce, their machinery and implements, and their skills. After passing close to the once busy Hucknall Aerodrome we return via woodland paths and farm lanes. The route twice crosses the motorway, but any consequent disturbance of the peace is soon left behind.

The Queen's Head

The exterior aspect of the Queen's Head immediately attracts, with its traditional appearance and pretty, colourful windowboxes. The interior décor is equally attractive, featuring timber-cladded walls and ceiling. An old building, with a pleasant, busy atmosphere, this is a Scottish and Newcastle house. Full meals and snacks are available throughout the week between 12 noon and 2 pm, and in the evening from 6 pm to 8 pm. The bill of fare offers traditional pies, fish and chips and so on, as well as a number of specials. Vegetarian options are also available, and the range of snacks includes rolls, baguettes and toasted sandwiches. Families are welcome in the dining area and the children's play facility forms a part of a most attractive enclosed garden area.

Lunchtime opening is from 11.30 am (12 noon on Sundays) until 3 pm; evenings from 5.30 pm to 11 pm in the week and 10.30 pm on Sundays. Telephone: 0115 938 3148.

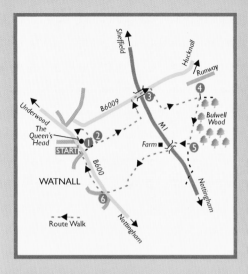

The Walk

① Leave the road just north of the pub, following a waymarked footpath between the houses. By a road junction, turn right along a gravelled track. Enter the bungalow gateway at the end, leaving again by a stile on the left. With your back to the stile, bear right over the field, passing between two great sycamore trees, to reach and pass through a metal farm gate.

② Turn left, joining the Robin Hood Way. Follow the edge of two fields, turning left at the far end to reach the road (B6009) and turn right, crossing the M1 motorway.

③ Leave the road again on reaching a farm track on the right, close to a bus shelter. Follow the clear track down the

Poppies

The path near the old aerodrome at Hucknall

centre of the vast field. Turn left where the track bends, reverting to a narrower footpath. Follow the wooded way alongside the perimeter of the Hucknall Aerodrome runway (now resting!).

④ Pass through a bridle gate and turn right, following the waymarked footpath as for Nuthall Cemetery. Follow the edge of Bulwell Wood, and onward, ignoring a spur path on the left.

⑤ On reaching a stile, turn right to join a farm track. Cross the motorway via the access bridge, continuing past Common Farm and on, through a small industrial estate, to reach the main (B600) road.

⑥ Turn right and continue back to the Queen's Head.

PLACES OF INTEREST NEARBY

The D. H. Lawrence Heritage at Durban House Heritage Centre, Mansfield Road, Eastwood, to the west of Watnall. Living history for all the family as they experience life as lived by the local author. Plus restaurant/coffee shop and craft workshops. For further information, including full brochure, telephone: 01773 717353.

Bagthorpe
The Shepherd's Rest

MAP: OS EXPLORER 269 (GR 467515)   **WALK 10**   **DISTANCE:** 3 MILES

DIRECTIONS TO START: BAGTHORPE LIES JUST NORTH OF UNDERWOOD AND CAN BE REACHED VIA JUNCTION 27 OF THE M1 AND THE A608 OR JUNCTION 26 AND THE B600. IN UNDERWOOD TURN NORTHWARDS ALONG CHURCH LANE. AT THE T-JUNCTION, TURN LEFT AND CONTINUE. THE SHEPHERD'S REST IS ON THE RIGHT. **PARKING:** THERE IS LIMITED PARKING AT THE PUB FOR PATRONS, SO PLEASE CONSULT THE PROPRIETORS BEFORE LEAVING YOUR VEHICLE HERE WHILST YOU WALK.

The tiny settlement of Bagthorpe, which forms part of the parish of Selston, rests by a quiet lane in a tranquil valley, an oasis of calm in the green belt. Walking these rural paths today, it is hard to imagine that, not so very long ago, these acres supported a flourishing coal industry, familiar to the great D. H. Lawrence, who declared this area to be the country of his heart.

After an initial crossing of Bagthorpe Brook, our stroll takes us via quiet ways to Underwood Green, from where we circle round by Wansley Hall, recrossing the brook and continuing to the outskirts of Selston. We return to Bagthorpe over fields which, in their time, were crossed by a mineral line and lay in the shadow of the pithead gear.

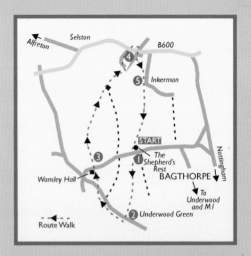

The Shepherd's Rest

The Shepherd's Rest, a Pub Enterprises (Scottish and Newcastle) house, sits at the foot of the hill in this quiet yet pretty backwater, providing peaceful relaxation in pleasant surroundings. All the popular facilities are here: a children's play area, as well as a non-alcoholic family room, an outside drinking area and non-smoking zones. Well-behaved dogs are also welcome. Meals and bar snacks are available at lunchtimes and in the evenings, and an exhaustive menu caters for everyone. Vegetarians, children and senior citizens will all find something to their taste here, as also will those who favour the more challenging traditional and exotic dishes. All food is freshly prepared upon receipt of the order. There is all day opening every day from 12 noon. Telephone: 01773 810506.

The Walk

① Leaving the pub, turn left along the road, then right, crossing the footbridge over the Bagthorpe Brook and continuing along an enclosed narrow footpath – what our children used to call a 'snicky path'. This alternates with open fields, where the path follows the left-hand hedge, and eventually leads out to a derelict farm area and, via an unmade track, to the road at Underwood Green.

② Turn right. Over the hill, descend past a road junction, enjoying the splendid distant views in front. Ignore the first footpath sign on the right, continuing on a little further to a second guidepost and

stile. Cross here – the access was a mite overgrown when the writer came – and go diagonally over the field, passing to the rear of the farm buildings, to reach the road by Wansley Hall.

③ Cross the road and continue down the fields. There is a timeless air about the field paths here, and it is easy to imagine oneself enjoying precisely the same views and sensations that Lawrence must have known, nearly a century ago. Cross Bagthorpe Brook again, continuing down the centre of an ensuing field. Over a second brook, the path, as shown on the map, branches (although that to the left may not be evident on the ground). Keep to the right here, with the hedge also on your right. Continue past Home Farm, keeping straight ahead along a gravelled road to the outskirts of Selston. Turn right along Lea Lane to reach Nottingham Road (B600), turning right again here.

④ Turn right once more at Sperry Close and continue on, to reach an enclosed footpath between nos 17 and 18. Follow this up the hill to reach 'Inkerman'; which

Our path near Inkerman

appears to consist of old miners' rows – the only visible reminder that this was once a mining community. The name, and that of 'Alma' close by, perhaps provides a clue to the antiquity of the little estate: the mid 19th century?

⑤ Where the road bends, keep straight on along the waymarked field path, maintaining the same line all the way back to Bagthorpe. A copy of an early Ordnance Survey (19th century) map of the area shows two mines in this area, and a mineral line crossing these fields. The beauty and tranquillity of the scene today provides no surviving evidence.

PLACES OF INTEREST NEARBY

Midland Railway Centre, Butterley Station, Ripley, over the border in Derbyshire, to the west of Bagthorpe. Many locomotives and items of rolling stock of Midland and LMS origin can be seen here and there is a steam-hauled passenger service, a museum site, and a country and farm park. Telephone: 01773 747674 for details of opening hours and admission charges.

Calverton
The Admiral Rodney

MAP: OS EXPLORER 260 (GR 613493) · **WALK 11** · **DISTANCE:** 3½ MILES

DIRECTIONS TO START: VIA THE A6097 (FOSSE WAY TO OXTON ROAD), TURNING OFF AT MOOR LANE, 1 MILE NORTH-WEST OF EPPERSTONE. THE PUB IS ON THE RIGHT IN MAIN STREET. **PARKING:** AT THE ADMIRAL RODNEY BUT, FOR SECURITY REASONS, PLEASE ADVISE PROPRIETORS BEFORE LEAVING YOUR VEHICLE. IF NOT USING THE PUB, IN ST WILFRID'S SQUARE, CALVERTON.

Calverton has long been a centre of Nottinghamshire's cottage hosiery industry, evidence of which is still to be seen in the specially designed windows for maximising the available daylight. Indeed, the village was the home, four centuries ago, of William Lee, the inventor of the stocking frame. In more recent years, the area has relied heavily on the coal industry, the local pit having been responsible, in the second half of the 20th century, for a seven-fold increase in the local population. But the heart of the village retains its rural ambience, and the surrounding fields and woods are a constant delight to the carefree wanderer.

After following the road out of Calverton, a quiet country lane leads up onto the wooded hills to the south of the village, where distant views delight the eye. The route follows the crest of the hills, passing the site of ancient earthworks, before descending along a pretty wooded path, back to the 'Rodney'.

The Admiral Rodney

The Admiral Rodney is a free house; a clean and cheerful traditional village inn, attractive both inside and out, with a friendly management. Families are welcome, and there is a large range of children's drinks. Dogs, too, are welcome in the public bar. Special arrangements, for parking and catering, will be made for coach parties of walkers, subject to prior notice.

There is all day opening from 11.30 am to 11 pm on Monday to Saturday. Sunday hours are from 12 noon to 3 pm and 7 pm to 10.30 pm. Food is served daily, both meals and bar snacks, and a full menu of main courses, sandwiches and snacks is supplemented by the usual 'blackboard' range of daily specials, with a choice of cask ales and speciality guest beers to wash it down. Telephone: 0115 847 1789.

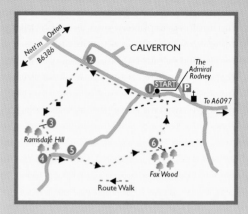

The Walk

① Follow Main Street west out of the village.

② Beyond the built-up area (opposite a sign pointing to Calverton Colliery), turn left into Hollinwood Lane, a roughly surfaced country road. Pass a golf course, on your left, and ascend gently to Hollinwood House, the entrance to which is barred by a vast wooden gate. Bear right of the gate, following a footpath along the perimeter of the property. Continue onto the fields, rich in summer with, among other flora, red campion and birds-eye – and buttercups galore.

③ Rejoin the roadway, here a broad rough track crossing the golf course with superb wide views back over the county. At the top of Ramsdale Hill, cross a stile on the right, leaving the golf course and turning left along a woodland track. Continue to the road.

④ Cross the road and turn left, following the road round the bend and keeping, for safety's sake, to the wide grass verge. Here again, there are wide views to be enjoyed, this time to the south.

Near Fox Wood

Hollinwood

⑤ Where the road bends sharp left, keep straight forward along the bridleway track. Bear left at a junction of paths, to continue ahead along an enclosed green lane, with Calverton visible below, on the left.

⑥ Beside Fox Wood, the site of an ancient hill-fort, look for a stile on the left, leading into a descending path beside the hedge. This in turn leads into a delightful wooded way, continuing down the hill towards the village. Turn left with the track, and right again at a crossways (Woods Lane) to reach Main Street, opposite the Admiral Rodney.

PLACES OF INTEREST NEARBY

Patching's Farm Art Centre, Oxton Road, Calverton – 60 acres of countryside incorporating a unique attraction, with gardens, galleries, pottery, textile and framing centres. Art and craft materials are on sale and there is a gift shop. Art courses are provided for all ages and abilities. Licensed restaurant. Admission free. Telephone: 0115 965 3479.

Woodborough
The Four Bells

MAP: OS EXPLORER 260 (GR 631478)   **WALK 12**   **DISTANCE:** 3½ MILES

DIRECTIONS TO START: FROM NOTTINGHAM CITY CENTRE, FOLLOW THE B684, TURNING RIGHT AT MAPPERLEY PLAINS. AN ALTERNATIVE APPROACH IS VIA THE A6097 BINGHAM TO OXTON ROAD, TURNING OFF WEST AT EPPERSTONE. THE PUB IS IN MAIN STREET, JUST WEST OF THE CHURCH. **PARKING:** AT THE FOUR BELLS (PATRONS ONLY) OR TIDILY, ON-STREET.

The pretty village of Woodborough lies amid gently rolling hills and fertile farmland, long a centre of the market gardening industry and, in former times, of cottage based framework knitting. One of Woodborough's more famous sons, the Rev George Brown, was born in the early 18th century to a family of framework knitters. The 13th century tower of the parish church of St Swithun used to have four bells (explaining the name of the 'local') which figured in a local rhyme:

> Calverton crack pancheons,
> Woodborough merry bells;
> Oxton ding-dongs,
> Lowdham eggshells

This walk takes us up over fertile fields between Woodborough and Lambley, before circling round along quiet country lanes – and more field paths – back to the Four Bells.

The Four Bells

You will find a warm and friendly welcome at the Four Bells, a picturesque country pub in a popular location, with well-tended gardens and a pleasant atmosphere. A Scottish and Newcastle house, home-made meals and snacks are provided at lunchtime daily, and in the evening from Monday to Saturday. There is an extensive snack menu embracing a variety of sandwiches, baguettes, light bites and jacket potatoes. The bill of fare for full meals changes daily, and is as listed on the bar blackboard. A traditional roast is available every Sunday, from noon until 5.30 pm.

Opening hours from Monday to Friday are from 11 am to 3 pm and 5 pm to 11 pm. There is all day opening at the weekend; round the clock from 11 am on Saturday and between 12 noon and 10.30 pm on Sunday. Families are welcome, and there is a children's playground, an outside drinking area, and no-smoking zones. Dogs are welcome, outside only. Telephone: 0115 965 6670.

The Walk

① Follow Main Street east, passing the church and following the road round by the Nag's Head. At the end of the village, turn right as directed by a guidepost, following the bridleway over a paddock and turning right on reaching a farm track. Bear left by the caravan site, onto a rough unmade track which continues as a hedgeside field path. Follow the path over several fields.

② Turn right at a guidepost and follow the track to the road. Turn right again, following the road round the leftward curve. Where the road bends sharp right, keep straight forward along a rough lane.

③ Turn right at a bridleway sign, along an enclosed pathway. Turn right again on reaching a footpath sign. Keep to the right of the hedge over three fields to reach Lingwood Lane – where a welcome seat will no doubt encourage you to linger.

Looking towards Ploughman Wood

Above Woodborough

④ Follow Lingwood Lane down the hill, back to Woodborough church, turning left here for the Four Bells.

PLACES OF INTEREST NEARBY

Playworld at Floralands Garden Centre, Catfoot Lane, Lambley. A 2 acre outdoor adventure play park for the children, with numerous exciting attractions, plus a special area for the under fives. Telephone: 0115 967 0487.

Lowdham
The Old Ship Inn

MAP: OS EXPLORER 260 (GR 669465)	WALK 13	DISTANCE: 3 MILES

DIRECTIONS TO START: THE VILLAGE OF LOWDHAM STANDS AT THE JUNCTION OF THE A612 (NOTTINGHAM/SOUTHWELL) AND A6097 (BINGHAM/OXTON) ROADS. THE TURNING FOR MAIN STREET WILL BE FOUND IMMEDIATELY TO THE EAST OF THE ROUNDABOUT, BESIDE THE MAGNA CARTA INN. **PARKING:** AT THE OLD SHIP (PATRONS ONLY) OR TIDILY, ON-STREET.

Two main roads cross at Lowdham, effectively splitting the community into four parts. Thus, the main village, the church and the railway station each occupy a different quarter. One advantage of the arrangement is that Main Street, having been reprieved by the construction, in the 1930s, of the A6097 bypass, is now restored to its proper status as a quiet, though lively thoroughfare. The village and its surroundings at one time boasted no fewer than ten corn mills, although only two now remain in the village itself. But Lowdham – a flourishing community – is still well served with shops and pubs.

Peaceful field paths circle around the lower slopes of Barker Hill, leading the walker to the tiny village of Gonalston, its prettiness today concealing a tragic two-centuries-old tale of child exploitation. The return journey follows a quiet tree-lined country lane, before descending via bridleway, beck and mill, back to Lowdham.

The Old Ship

The proprietors claim (and who am I to dispute the matter?) that their Ship is the furthest from the sea in the UK. Be that as it may, it is certainly one ship that has grown in size, having taken on board the adjacent cottages; despite which it still retains all the atmosphere of a friendly, typical village inn, with obliging staff and cheery clientele. This is a free house, including among the beverages John Smith's Bitter and Strongbow cider. Full meals and bar snacks are available daily on Monday to Saturday from noon until 2 pm and in the evening between 6 pm and 9.30 pm. Sunday lunch is also provided, from noon until 2.30 pm. The bill of fare is impressive and all food is freshly prepared to order. (And the ploughman's filled rolls are positively the best I have tasted!).

Bed and breakfast can be obtained here and there are four en-suite rooms. Opening hours are from 11.30 am to 2.30 pm and 5.30 pm to 11 pm on Monday to Friday, 11.30 am to 11 pm on Saturday and 12 noon until 10.30 pm on Sunday. Telephone: 0115 966 3049.

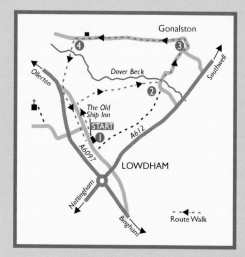

The Walk

① Follow Main Street north from the Old Ship. Opposite the school, turn right into Mount Pleasant, a rough track (waymarked as a footpath to Gonalston). Cross a stile and continue ahead, following the field path to the right of the hedge. The way reverts to the left of the hedge (ignore a clear cattle track bearing left), continuing straight ahead via the stiled path to emerge finally at a bend in a lane.

② Joining the lane, keep straight forward, with a cottage (The Hermitage) on your left. Continue to a road junction on the outskirts of Gonalston, one of the county's prettiest little villages and one of the least spoilt. The walk continues straight ahead, but you may consider it worth diverting to the right here, to explore the village before continuing. In the closing years of the 18th century, the local cotton mill (nowadays, a private residence) was the scene of some of the most diabolical exploitation of children. Orphans as young as seven years old were apprenticed to the millowner, working 14 to 16 hours a day, enduring regular thrashings and inadequate food. When this mill closed the apprentices were transferred to the notorious Litton Mill in Derbyshire – where an even more cruel regime operated.

③ Returning to the road junction, keep straight forward, negotiating a double leftward bend (and enjoying the 'song'

Car Holt Farm

of woodpigeon and rook) and following Gonalston Lane, a pleasant, tree-lined country road with very little traffic to bother you. But keep to the right all the same, just in case.

④ Past Car Holt Farm, turn left by a guidepost, following a public bridleway. Cross the Dover Beck and continue over a second bridge by Lowdham Mill (with mallard on the mill stream). Turn left at Epperstone road, following the secondary road back to the Old Ship.

PLACES OF INTEREST NEARBY

Ferry Farm Country Park, Boat Lane, Hoveringham (off the A612 between Lowdham and Southwell). Farmyard animals, rare breeds, pets' corner, wildlife pond, assault course, plus a gift shop and tearoom. Telephone: 0115 966 5037.

Farndon
The Rose and Crown

MAP: OS EXPLORER 271 (GR 770517)   **WALK 14**   **DISTANCE:** $3\frac{1}{2}$ MILES

DIRECTIONS TO START: FARNDON IS SITUATED ON THE WEST SIDE OF THE A46 (FOSSE WAY), ABOUT 2 MILES SOUTH-WEST OF NEWARK. THE ROSE AND CROWN IS ON MAIN STREET, IN THE CENTRE OF THE VILLAGE. **PARKING:** AT THE ROSE AND CROWN. FOR THOSE NOT VISITING THE PUB, THERE IS A PUBLIC CAR PARK BY THE RIVERSIDE, ABOUT $\frac{1}{4}$ MILE FURTHER ON.

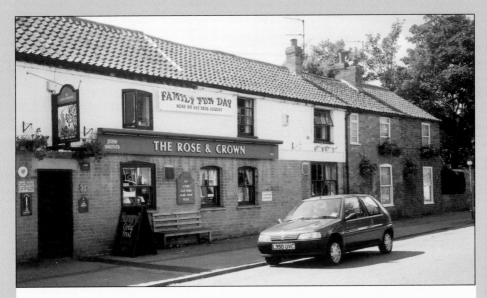

A harbour is not a feature one normally expects to find some seventy or eighty miles inland; so one wonders how many motorists, driving along the Fosse Way to Newark, have done a 'double-take' on spotting a sign pointing the way to 'Farndon Harbour'? In this case, the harbour is the local marina, a busy little basin developed on the site of worked out gravel pits. There used to be a ferry here too, but that is something else that has vanished. But the river is still an attraction, with its anglers, pleasure craft and wildlife, and a waterside bridleway for the enjoyment of walkers and riders.

The walk described here follows the riverside path around a wide loop, almost, but not quite, describing a full circle. The final stage skirts the north-western fringe of Farndon, passing beside the Harbour to reach the public car park.

The Rose and Crown

The Rose and Crown is a traditional style village pub with low beams and tiled floors, in the centre of the village. This welcoming Scottish and Newcastle house has a secluded beer garden at the rear. And a play area for the children, families (and dogs) being welcome here. Food is served daily, from a standard menu which includes such favourites as steak and gravy pie, rump steak, sausage and mash and chicken tikka masala. Bar snacks include a full range of light bites, rolls, burgers and jacket potatoes. And an economically priced two-course lunch is available on Sundays, alongside the full menu.

The pub is open all day, every day; from 11 am in the week and from 12 noon on Sundays. Telephone: 01636 704334.

The Walk

Note: This route is negotiable by wheelchairs, with care; but a diversion, adding ³/₄ mile, is likely to be necessary between points 5 and 6.

① Turn left from the pub, following Main Street, Chapel Lane and Wyke Lane to the public car park.

② Walk through the Britannia Inn car park and past the New Ferry Restaurant, to join and follow the riverside path downstream. Cross the Farndon Harbour footbridge and continue along the former towpath, ignoring a footpath turning on the right.

③ The river curves round to the right

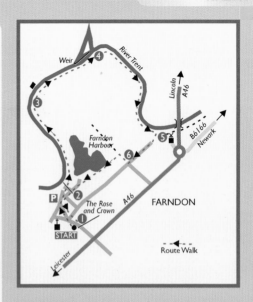

opposite Staythorpe Power Station; now greatly reduced in scale with little more than a single brick building to interrupt the view or disturb the peace. As you proceed, look out ahead, and to the right, for the spire of Newark parish church. And enjoy the occasional passing river cruiser, narrow boat or canoeist, and the various forms of wildfowl upon the river and its banks.

④ The river branches at Averham (pronounced 'Air-um') Weir. The northern arm, which is un-navigable, flows via Kelham, bypassing Newark. The path remains with the Newark arm, taking a further bend to the right, after which the arable fields give place to pleasant riverside meadows.

⑤ On reaching a windmill (no sails), turn sharp right, following an enclosed public footpath. Continue ahead into a housing estate and turn right at a mini-roundabout (the junction with Long Lane).

The River Trent at Farndon

Wheelchairs: The enclosed footpath referred to above is equipped with a form of barrier, which may prevent wheelchairs from passing. In this event, the shortest route (adding $^3/_4$ mile) is to continue beside the river, passing under the A46 bridge and turning right along another footpath. This leads to the B6166. Turn right here, passing the 'Lord Ted' pub and continuing round the roundabout and on along the A46 towards Farndon. Turn right at Long Lane, joining the main route by the mini-roundabout and continuing straight forward.

⑥ Where this road swings left, keep on ahead, following the gravelled lane, then turn left at a guideposted side turning. Pass the marina, following the pathway over Farndon Wildflower Meadow.

Continue via North End to Wyke Lane, turning right here, back to the public car park, Chapel Lane and the Rose and Crown.

PLACES OF INTEREST NEARBY

Newark Castle – historic ruins, dating back to the early 12th century and occupying a commanding position overlooking the River Trent. The grounds are open to the public daily, from dawn to dusk; admission free. A small charge is made for public guided tours of the castle, bookings for which are taken at the Tourist Information Centre. In the adjoining Gilstrap Centre, the Newark Castle Story exhibition tells the fascinating history of the castle. Telephone: 01636 655765.

Edingley
The Old Reindeer

MAP: OS EXPLORER 28 (270) (GR 664560)   **WALK 15**   **DISTANCE:** $3\frac{1}{2}$ MILES

DIRECTIONS TO START: EDINGLEY IS NORTH-WEST OF SOUTHWELL ON THE UNCLASSIFIED ROAD TO RAINWORTH AND MANSFIELD. IF APPROACHING EASTWARDS FROM THE A614 (WHITE POST ROUNDABOUT) FOLLOW THE UNCLASSIFIED ROAD FOR $2\frac{1}{2}$ MILES, PASSING THROUGH FARNSFIELD, TO REACH EDINGLEY. THE OLD REINDEER IS IN THE CENTRE OF THE VILLAGE. **PARKING:** AT THE OLD REINDEER, (PATRONS ONLY), OR ON THE ROADSIDE BY THE CHURCH.

Edingley hides its light under a bushel. One of our local guidebooks describes it simply as 'a trim little village', which is true enough. Tucked away in the orchard area of central Notts on the quiet road between Farnsfield and Southwell, with the Southwell Trail to the north, a tasty ridge of hills to the south, and the eponymous Beck flowing between the two, this is an attractive, and sadly understated, area. There were working mills around Edingley in the past, including at least one cotton mill, as immortalised in the name of a farm and a dyke. And the local footpaths and byways make for easy walking.

Quiet country lanes, byways and footpaths are the hallmark of this enjoyable stroll over rolling hills. The only serious climbing – a gentle road incline – is disposed of in the early stages, after which the challenges arise solely from some tightish stiles.

The Old Reindeer

One of Wolverhampton and Dudley Breweries' houses, the Old Reindeer is a friendly and welcoming 18th century village pub. Interesting features in the bar include a stag's head – left behind, presumably, by the old reindeer – and an intriguing collection of 'gozunders' (potties, to you!). All those special facilities are here: family room, children's play area, beer garden and non-smoking areas (and, when we came, two ponies). And well-behaved dogs are welcome. Meals and bar snacks are served daily; between 12 noon and 3 pm on Tuesday to Sunday and from 7 pm until 10 pm on Monday to Saturday. There is no standard menu, and the range changes daily, as displayed on the bar blackboard.

Opening hours are from 11 am to 3 pm on Tuesday to Friday, 5.30 pm to 11 pm on Monday to Friday evening and all day opening (12 noon until 11 pm) on Saturday and Sunday. The pub is closed Monday lunchtime. Telephone: 01623 882253.

The Walk

① Follow Main Street in the direction of Southwell. On the right, just past the junction with Station Road, leave the road via a waymarked footpath on the right, passing along the driveway of Razway Cottage and continuing diagonally over two fields to reach Greaves Lane. Turn right.

② Turn left at the road junction (Little Hill), ascending to a T-junction. Turn right here, climbing steadily and easily for

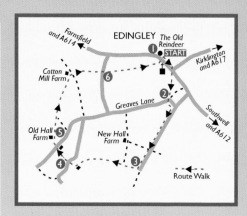

½ mile. Ignore a crossways at the first summit, with the access to New Hall Farm on the right. Continue downhill and up again to the second summit.

③ Turn right, following a pleasant green lane, on the route of the Robin Hood Way. Continue past Little Turncroft Farm and turn left at the road.

④ Go right at a guidepost, crossing the stile and descending over two fields to a farm (a stile to the left of the buildings) and Greaves Lane. Cross the road and bear right over the field, as directed by the guidepost. Follow the edge of a pond and stream up to the top of the next field; cross the stile and turn left, initially along a farm track, but keeping as close as

PLACES OF INTEREST NEARBY

Wonderland Pleasure Park, White Post, Farnsfield – 30 acres of parkland with a large tropical house, home to exotic butterflies, insects and fish. There is an indoor soft play area, an outdoor adventure play area and scores of other attractions for the family. Open daily, all through the year. Telephone: 01623 882773.

The view towards Cotton Mill Farm

convenient to the hedge on the right as you continue over the field.

⑤ Cross a stile on the right and continue straight ahead over a series of fields. Entering a farm lane (the access to Cotton Mill Farm), continue ahead over a stile. There are two stiles on the right immediately after this one. Ignore the first, and cross the second, to follow the footpath along the fieldside, with Cotton Mill Dyke on your right. Continue to Allesford Lane.

⑥ Cross the road and continue over the fields. Keep straight ahead, ignoring a left turn in an intervening length of farm road, to emerge onto an access road beside Edingley village church. Join Main Street and turn left.

Blidworth Bottoms
The Fox and Hounds

MAP: OS EXPLORER 28 (270) (GR 590548)   **WALK 16**   **DISTANCE:** 3 MILES

DIRECTIONS TO START: BLIDWORTH BOTTOMS LIES SOUTH OF BLIDWORTH VILLAGE AND THE B6020. APPROACHING FROM THE A614 IN THE SOUTH, FOLLOW THE UNCLASSIFIED BLIDWORTH LANE (SIGNED FOR BLIDWORTH BOTTOMS) NORTH-WEST FOR 1½ MILES. THE FOX AND HOUNDS IS ON THE RIGHT, OPPOSITE A ROAD JUNCTION. **PARKING:** AT THE FOX AND HOUNDS (PATRONS ONLY) OR – HALF A MILE OFF-ROUTE, AT FOREST PARKING AREA, BLIDWORTH LANE (GR 595643).

Blidworth is the undisputed home of much of the Robin Hood tradition. The birthplace, we are told, of Maid Marian and the final resting-place of Will Scarlet. And Robin's first ignominious encounter with the doughty Friar Tuck took place in nearby Fountains Dale. Some will say that Robin Hood is only a legend – though no trueborn son of Nottinghamshire would dare confess to such a heresy. Blidworth today is an area of fertile farms, rolling hills and glorious woodland. And perfect strolling country.

Blidworth Bottoms, where the walk begins, is no more than a hamlet. It is a walk in three distinct stages, starting first with about a mile of road-walking. We then cross a series of arable fields to reach the main hilltop village of Blidworth, before returning to the start via a gently declining unmade rural lane.

The Fox and Hounds

The Fox and Hounds started life as a farmhouse. A cosy rural pub, the house is said to have had associations with the celebrated Lord Byron, whose Newstead home was not so far away from here. This is a Kimberley house, with a family room and a pleasant grassy outside drinking area. Food is available every lunchtime and evening except Monday, and there is a mouthwatering selection of traditional fare, alongside a few more exotic modern dishes. Vegetarians are catered for, as are the children, and fresh filled rolls are prepared to order.

Lunchtime opening is from 12 noon until 2.30 pm on Tuesday to Friday and 3 pm at the weekend. Evenings from 6 pm until 11 pm except Sunday (10.30 pm closing) and Monday (closed all day). Telephone: 01623 792383.

The Walk

① With your back to the pub, turn right and follow the road, passing the Blidworth turning and continuing ahead for about a mile. This is not a very busy road, but there is no pavement, so keep well into the right to avoid any oncoming traffic.

② Turn right at the B6020 (opposite the Fairview Riding School), following the footpath along the grass verge. Cross a

Meadow Cranesbill

Beck Lane, Blidworth

stile on the right, joining the field path. A well-trodden footpath crosses a series of fields of fertile arable land on the route of the Robin Hood Way, with superb rural views over the surrounding countryside.

③ Turn left at Field Lane, ascending the hill to Blidworth village. Turn right at the Black Bull, following the main street past the White Lion.

④ Turn right again at Beck Lane (by the public telephone box). Over the brow of the hill, the road reverts to an unmade lane – sometimes gravel, sometimes sand – descending easily to Blidworth Bottoms (Kirkfield Equestrian Centre).

⑤ Turn right, and follow the road back to the Fox and Hounds.

PLACES OF INTEREST NEARBY

The Longdale Craft Centre, on Longdale Lane, Ravenshead (south of Blidworth) is reputed to be Britain's oldest rural craft centre, incorporating workshops, a museum and a gallery. Crafts include a framing service, jewellery, wood, sculpture and ceramics, with resident craft-persons at work. There is parking for coaches and cars, and group bookings are welcome. Open all day, every day. Telephone: 01623 794858.

Forest Town
The Whitegates Hotel

MAP: OS EXPLORER 28 (270) (GR 572627)   **WALK 17**   **DISTANCE:** $3\frac{1}{2}$ MILES

DIRECTIONS TO START: FOREST TOWN IS ON THE NORTH-EAST SIDE OF MANSFIELD, ON THE B6030. APPROACHING FROM THE A614 NOTTINGHAM TO OLLERTON ROAD, NORTH OF RUFFORD, FOLLOW THE B6030 THROUGH OLD AND NEW CLIPSTONE. THE WHITEGATES HOTEL IS A LARGE MODERN BUILDING ON THE LEFT, OPPOSITE THE JUNCTION WITH CLIPSTONE DRIVE. **PARKING:** AT THE WHITEGATES HOTEL OR, TIDILY, ON CLIPSTONE DRIVE.

Forest Town is a suburb of Mansfield, but probably has a greater affinity with the mining town of New Clipstone, its close neighbour to the east. But the name is distinctive; and appropriate, for it lies in the heart of the ancient Sherwood Forest. And, as the following stroll will show, the forest is still very much a part of the local environment. Mansfield itself is one of the county's major towns, and takes its name from the River Maun, which flows through the town.

The Maun also passes close by Forest Town, and this exhilarating little walk – in keeping with the name – remains, once the built-up area is left behind, entirely within the forest lands and beside the Maun and its fisheries.

The Whitegates Hotel

The Whitegates, a large and solidly-built modern building, stands on the boundary between New Clipstone and Forest Town, drawing patronage from both communities. Meals and bar snacks are served. The food consists mainly of traditional English dishes (such as Toad in the Hole), and the traditional Sunday lunch is available in both large and small versions. Bar snacks include a selection of cobs, hot baguettes and jacket potatoes. This is one of Samuel Smith's houses, open from 11.30 am to 3 pm and 5.30 pm to 11 pm on Monday to Friday, with all day opening on Saturday from 11.30 am to 11 pm and on Sunday from 12 noon until 11 pm. Food is served daily, from 12 noon until 2 pm throughout the week; also in the evening, Monday to Friday only, between 5.30 pm and 7.45 pm. Families are welcome and there is a children's play area. Telephone: 01623 624689.

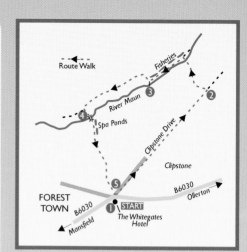

The Walk

Note: Accessible with wheelchairs and baby buggies.

① Cross the road, join and follow Clipstone Drive out of the built-up area, continuing ahead along the unmetalled way through the forest.

② At the end of a block of conifers, turn left onto a waymarked track and descend to the River Maun. Turn left, following the track between the river and the fishing ponds (Maun Fisheries). A most pleasant spot this, with the charmingly landscaped ponds utilising the flood dike, and providing endless sport for the angler.

③ At the end of the fisheries, follow the track round to the right, past the gate and up the incline. Turn left again at the top of the rise, following a quiet rural pathway above the Maun valley.

Spa Ponds

Maun Fisheries

④ Turn left again at a crossing of the ways, descending to recross the Maun and continuing into the forest. Follow the woodland path past the Spa Ponds, a series of four ponds, three of them medieval, which are maintained as a nature reserve by the Nottinghamshire Wildlife Trust and are host to a variety of wildfowl and insect life. Continue on and ascend, keeping to the right at a junction of paths, back to Clipstone Drive.

⑤ Turn right.

PLACES OF INTEREST NEARBY

Mansfield Museum and Art Gallery, Leeming Lane, Mansfield. Features include local, social and natural history exhibits. Open Monday to Saturday, admission free. Telephone: 01623 463088.

Norwell
The Plough

MAP: OS EXPLORER 271 (GR 770616)   **WALK 18**   **DISTANCE:** $2^3/_4$ MILES

DIRECTIONS TO START: VIA THE A1 TO THE CROMWELL BYPASS, TURNING OFF HERE INTO CROMWELL VILLAGE, THEN WEST FOR NORWELL. THE PUB IS IN MAIN STREET. **PARKING:** AT THE PLOUGH (PATRONS ONLY). APART FROM ON-STREET PARKING, THERE IS ALSO LIMITED ROADSIDE SPACE ON THE RIGHT, PAST THE CHURCH.

An unassuming little village, the name of Norwell (the local pronunciation is Norral) is a corruption of Northwell – as opposed to the more upmarket Southwell. Once a prosperous town with a fair and a weekly market, there are the moated sites of two manor houses still within the village precincts, and another three in the area. The village remains largely unaffected by modern developments; there are a number of 17th/18th century houses, and the church of St Lawrence is of impressive size for such a small place. The 19th century windmill has lost its cap and sails, but the unusual circular brick pinfold, of late 18th or early 19th century vintage, is still to be seen.

A straightforward little saunter takes us out via the Cromwell road and over the local waterway, after which we join a bridleway, circling round parallel to the beck, before returning along a quiet by-lane to Norwell village.

The Plough

Originally three separate cottages, the Plough is a really attractive and cosy traditional village pub, with the essential features of low-beamed ceilings, lots of brassware and some splendid old local views. The age of the house is uncertain, but the list of licensees dates back over a hundred years – and the general appearance of the pub suggests a much greater age. For good measure, there are rumours of a ghost – although the newly installed landlord had not yet made its acquaintance when I visited, and could not provide any details. It is a Pubmaster's pub and ales include Tetleys, Carlsberg, Greene King IPA and Murphys. Also Dry Blackthorn cider and Stella Artois.

The pub does not open at lunchtime, except on Saturday and Sunday, when the hours are from 12 noon until 3 pm. Evening opening, throughout the week, is from 7 pm until 11 pm. Food is served from 12 noon until 2 pm at the weekend, and in the evening, Tuesday to Saturday, between 7 pm and 9 pm. All food is cooked to order, so patience is the watchword if delays occur. The menu is staggering in its diversity, with a comprehensive selection of soups, starters, main courses and sweets, not to mention a choice of filled rolls and snack foods, a children's menu and a full Sunday lunch menu – subject to advance booking. Telephone: 01636 636208.

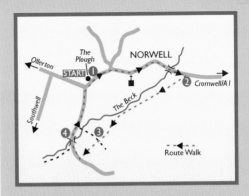

The Walk

① Follow Main Street east through the village, passing the church and continuing along the Cromwell road. Cross Beck Bridge.

② Turn right at a guidepost, following the waymarked public bridleway, a clear farm track. The track crosses from the right of the hedge to the left, in the second field; then, after a brief unfenced section, reverts to the right. Follow the hedge round the end of the field to pass through a gap and continue on the diverted route beside the Beck. (This is not the line shown on the most recent maps, which appear, on this point, to be well out of date!).

PLACES OF INTEREST NEARBY
The Bramley Apple Exhibition: H. Merryweather and Sons Ltd, Halam Road, Southwell. The exhibition, incorporated in the Garden Centre, tells the story of the world-famous apple. Open daily from 9 am to 5 pm. Admission free. Telephone: 01636 813204.

Norwell

③ Turn right at a waymarked junction of paths; then left at a second junction. Continue to a minor road and turn right.

④ Cross the Beck and pass Watermill Cottage, continuing ahead to Norwell.

Sutton on Trent
The Memory Lane

MAP: OS EXPLORER 271 (GR 800655) **WALK 19** **DISTANCE:** 2¾ MILES

DIRECTIONS TO START: IF TRAVELLING FROM THE NEWARK DIRECTION, FOLLOW THE A1 ROAD NORTH TO CARLTON ON TRENT. JOIN THE B1164 (THE 'OLD' A1) HERE AND CONTINUE FOR 1½ MILES TO SUTTON. THE TURNING FOR MAIN STREET IS OFF TO THE EAST. TRAVELLERS FROM THE NORTH SHOULD JOIN THE B1164 AT TUXFORD. **PARKING:** THE MEMORY LANE CAR PARK (PATRONS ONLY) OR, TIDILY, ON-STREET.

The re-routing of the A1 road away from Sutton has relieved the village of the bane of heavy traffic and, at the same time, created something of a barrier against extensive development on its western flanks. With the low-lying nature of the land to the east already preventing any development on that side, this has allowed the village to maintain its traditional style and its air of quietude. The riverside meadows include 300 acres of unfenced grazing (the Holmes) which are let each year to various 'gait-holders', each gait representing one beast. The annual gait-letting takes place in the spring, the successful bidders being permitted to graze cattle on the Holmes from May to December, according to the number of gaits allocated.

An easy stroll crosses the home meadows to reach the riverside Holmes, continuing along the riverside path where we find peaceful enjoyment of the pastoral scene.

The Memory Lane

The Memory Lane is a traditional village free house which has been refurbished on a 'Walk down Memory Lane' theme, offering a comfortable bar area, together with a non-smoking lounge and restaurant. A barn conversion provides en-suite accommodation, together with a conservatory and bar which is ideal for meetings and small functions, and there is also an attractive outdoor drinking area and children's play area. Food is available lunchtime and evenings, and a comprehensive menu spans the entire range from light lunchtime bites to full three course meals. Specialities include the frequently changing Chef's Specials, the traditional desserts menu and the senior citizens' menu. And the 'Sunday lunches' (traditional roast or vegetarian) are so popular that they are served every day.

Opening hours on Monday to Friday are from 12 noon until 2.30 pm and in the evening from 6 pm until 11 pm. There is all day opening from noon at the weekend, until 11 pm on Saturday and 10.30 pm on Sunday. Telephone: 01636 821071.

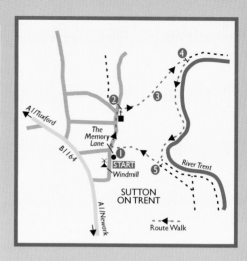

The Walk

① Follow Main Street north, continuing along Church Street, passing the parish church and entering Ingram Lane.

② Turn right at a guidepost by a farm, following the waymarked footpath beside the floodwall. Cross the wall, and a dyke, and bear left over the fields (perhaps to the accompaniment of chirping grasshoppers) upon a well-used path with good solid stiles.

③ Reaching the Holmes – the open grazing lands – the way becomes less clear; but you will need to be a dedicated failure to get lost here. Keep straight on to the riverside and turn right.

④ A pleasant pastoral spot, this, to rest awhile and enjoy the peacefulness of the broad, gently-flowing river with its occasional passing craft, cattle grazing, or ruminating, on the far bank, and perhaps an angler or two drowning worms. Follow the riverside path right and left around succeeding bends.

PLACES OF INTEREST NEARBY

The Vina Cooke Museum of Dolls and Bygone Childhood, at The Old Rectory, Cromwell (south of Sutton on Trent) has thousands of dolls, toys, prams and costumes on display, as well as a dolls' hospital, shop and tearoom. Groups are welcome, by appointment, and there is partial access for the disabled. Telephone: 01636 821364.

The River Trent at Sutton

⑤ After passing a pond, on your right – a former channel of the river, perhaps? – turn sharp right along a broad gravelled track. Follow this through to Sutton (Far Holme Lane) and turn left, onto Main Street.

Besthorpe
The Lord Nelson

| MAP: OS EXPLORER 271 (GR 826648) | **WALK 20** | DISTANCE: 3$\frac{1}{4}$ MILES |

DIRECTIONS TO START: BESTHORPE IS 2 MILES NORTH OF COLLINGHAM ON THE A1133 GAINSBOROUGH ROAD. THE LORD NELSON IS ON THE WEST SIDE OF THE MAIN ROAD. **PARKING:** AT THE LORD NELSON (PATRONS ONLY) OR, TIDILY, AROUND LOW STREET AREA.

Besthorpe is one of those tiny villages which, for the majority of motorists, other than those visiting the pub, is passed almost without recognition – and missed completely if the passer-by happens to blink. And a charming little village it is, with a village green, a church, a school, a modernised village hall and a large playing field; altogether, a range of facilities which many larger communities would envy. Many of the surrounding fields have been excavated for gravel, but the abandoned workings have been developed sympathetically, with nature reserves and a heronry which, with the waters of the River Fleet (formerly a section of the Trent), provide abundant interest for the rambler and countrygoer.

We follow the footpath way over the fields to the west of Besthorpe, continuing via broad acres of former quarry lands, much of it now restored to agricultural use or converted to newer, more environmentally diverse, uses. Our return journey skirts Girton old village before following the banks of the Fleet – at its widest here – back to Besthorpe.

The Lord Nelson

There is a pleasing old world atmosphere (and pistols over the bar) at the Lord Nelson, a free house and former coaching inn dating back over two hundred years. Overnight accommodation is available here, and food is served – bar snacks and full meals – each evening from Tuesday to Sunday and lunchtimes from Wednesday to Sunday. A varied menu, which includes fresh fish and game in season and a traditional Sunday lunch, is prepared on the premises.

Lunchtime opening is from 12 noon until 2 pm on Wednesday to Saturday and noon until 3 pm on Sunday. Evenings from 6 pm to 11 pm on Monday to Saturday and 7 pm to 10.30 pm on Sunday. The pub is closed at lunchtime on Monday and Tuesday. Telephone: 01636 892265.

The Walk

① Turn right towards Collingham, then right again at the first turning, into the village. Bear right a little by the green, continuing ahead on the side road and passing the church and the village hall. On along the farm drive (Fleet House Farm) and over the stile. Follow the field path, with the main arm of the Fleet on your right; cross another stile and continue, via the flood bank, over a second field to a third stile. Pass through an overgrown hedge and turn left along the side of a field, between hedge and ditch, to reach a field lane.

② Turn right along the lane, which soon bends left and right. A guidepost at the

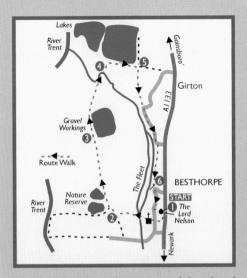

first bend points the way straight ahead over the fields, but there was no evidence when we came of any footpath; the logical conclusion being that the path is diverted around both bends of the lane. Continue this way, initially with a nature reserve, and later with arable fields, on the left, and with the cooling towers of High Marnham Power Station visible in the distance ahead.

③ On reaching a gate (the entrance to gravel workings, with no public access), keep left, following the path diversion alongside the hedge. Beyond the workings, the path resumes its traditional course. Go through the gate, bearing right a little from your former direction of travel and following a faint pathway around the field to arrive at a gated bridge over the Fleet. The latest edition of the OS map still indicates the presence of an oaken floodgate here, but all that seems to remain is a single upright post beside the inlet.

④ Cross the bridge and continue ahead to

The River Fleet

the junction with Trent Lane. Turn right and follow the lane, with fleeting glimpses of a vast recreational lake – former gravel workings – visible through the roadside hedge.

⑤ Right again at a crossways – a massive electricity pylon marks the spot – joining the line of the Trent Valley Way. A pleasant green way leads towards Girton village. Bypass the village on its right, rejoining the road at its southern limit. Follow the unfenced road for some distance, leaving it again on a leftward bend, in favour of a farm track. The Fleet is prominent on the right here, the width of this stretch giving credibility to its origin as a former channel of the Trent. Where the path branches, keep left,

ascending the flood bank to reach a small caravan site.

⑥ Through the hand-gate, follow the footpath round to the road and Besthorpe village. Keep straight forward, as far as a waymarked footpath on the left. Follow this through to the main (A1133) road and turn right.

PLACES OF INTEREST NEARBY
The Pureland Relaxation and Meditation Centre at North Clifton, a few miles north of Besthorpe, incorporates a beautiful and inspiring Japanese garden created by one man – the Buddhist monk Maitreya – out of a single derelict field. For fuller details, including opening hours and admission charges, telephone 01777 228567.

Edwinstowe
The Robin Hood

MAP: OS EXPLORER 28 (270) (GR 633655)   **WALK 21**   **DISTANCE:** 3³/₄ MILES

DIRECTIONS TO START: THE ROBIN HOOD STANDS ON THE JUNCTION OF THE B6030 AND B6034 ROADS, BOTH OF WHICH ARE ACCESSED FROM THE A614, SOUTH OF OLLERTON. **PARKING:** AT THE ROBIN HOOD. ALTERNATIVELY, FOR THOSE NOT USING THE PUB, IN RUFFORD PARK (SUBJECT TO A SMALL CHARGE).

Edwinstowe takes its name from Edwin, King of Northumbria, who died in battle on 12th October AD 632. Local legend has it that the village developed around the spot where his body had rested, and on which the parish church was built. Edwinstowe owes much of its present size to its more recent mining history, but its fame throughout the world today stems more from its reputation as the home of Robin Hood. Not necessarily where he was born, but certainly the heartland of all the legends; and, reputedly, the place where Robin and his Marian were wed, in the parish church of St Mary. The Major Oak is here, which some link with the outlaw band, although such claims need to be taken with a considerable helping of salt. But let us not pour scorn on all the legends. Our Robin is rightly celebrated here, and the Country Park and Visitor Centre well repay an hour or two of anyone's time.

On this occasion, however, we ignore the haunts of the worthy outlaws, to take a gentle stroll over to the east, where we visit a different Country Park – Rufford, with its beautiful lake and woodlands and its ruined Cistercian abbey/country house.

The Robin Hood

What better name could there be for a licensed house in the heart of Sherwood Forest? Although nominally in Edwinstowe, the pub lies outside the village itself, occupying a more rural setting halfway between Edwinstowe and Rufford. This is a large, modern building, one of Mansfield Brewery's (Wolverhampton and Dudley) houses; rather more of a tourist pub than most of our selection, but not necessarily any the worse for that. Families are welcome here, and there is a beer garden and a children's play area. Food is served, bar snacks and full meals, and the visitor will no doubt not be surprised to find that the menu includes such intriguing delights as Robin's Grill, Tuck's Sirloin, Scarlet Chicken – and Little John's Big Rump! Fish is a speciality, and various vegetarian dishes are also on offer.

Opening hours in the week are from 12 noon to 3 pm and 6 pm to 11 pm, with all day opening on Sundays. Telephone: 01623 822359.

The Walk

Note: This route should be found wheelchair-negotiable throughout.

① From the pub, turn left along Clipstone Road. Opposite the South Forest complex turn left again, onto the waymarked bridleway. Cross the corner of Broadoak Brake, turning left and right again with the track and continuing over the field towards the distant woods.

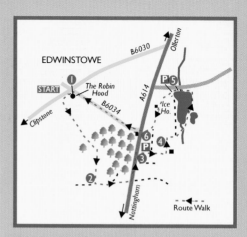

② On reaching a T-junction, turn left along the track, continuing for a short distance along the Center Parcs (Sherwood Holiday Village) access drive, but keeping straight forward, on the woodland bridleway, where the driveway bends left again. At the road (A614) cross over and turn left, following the paved path. Ignore the first turning, at the top of the rise, and continue to the next, the Rufford Park access.

③ Follow the access drive, passing the car park, to reach the Rufford Abbey buildings. The history of Rufford dates back beyond the Norman Conquest and it has in its time served as the estate of Gilbert de Gaunt, a nephew of the Conqueror, as a Cistercian abbey and, since the dissolution of the monasteries,

PLACES OF INTEREST NEARBY

Sherwood Pines Forest Park, The Forestry Commission, Sherwood Forest District, Edwinstowe – access from Clipstone Road, B6030. Waymarked walks and cycle rides (and cycle hire). Children's play-trail suitable for all abilities. Visitor Centre with shop, and freshly cooked food. Telephone: 01623 822447.

Beside Rufford lake

boardwalk round to reach Rufford Mill with its adjacent ford, and the Wellow road car park.

⑤ Cross the car park and follow the signposted track for the Woodland Walks. Pass the Broad Ride (on your left) keeping to the main track and ignoring, for the time being, all side turnings. Some way along, you will come to the 'Ice House' where, before the age of the fridge, ice used to be stored for the 'big house' through the summer. It was still in use as recently as 1936, but now serves purely as a historical curiosity. A second ice house, rather more neglected, might be found by diligent searching, in the woodlands behind this one. If you manage to find it, give yourself a pat on the back.

To continue the walk (from the first ice house) walk along the same track until you reach a broad ride on the right; a red and white Woodland Walks marker and a yellow footpath arrow mark the point. Turn off here and follow the ride through to the A614, opposite Rose Cottage.

⑥ Cross the road and follow the B6034 back to the Robin Hood.

as a private residence. After remaining in the hands of the Savile family for three centuries, the estate was purchased by the Notts County Council in 1961. The park itself, with its woodland walks and beautiful lake, is justly popular, and the stable block contains refreshments, a craft centre, a souvenir shop and toilets.

④ Turn left by the stable block, passing the abbey buildings and following the pathway round two sides of the grassed area. Turn left then, following the path along beside the field (a flock of rare breed Mouflon sheep are sometimes to be seen here). Keep right at a junction of paths, following the lakeside. A delightful section this, with lots of waterfowl. Any youngsters in the party will insist on 'feeding the ducks' – so come prepared! At the top end of the lake, follow the

Egmanton
The Old Plough Inn

MAP: OS EXPLORER 271 (GR 735688) **WALK 22** **DISTANCE:** 3 MILES

DIRECTIONS TO START: EGMANTON, WEST OF THE A1, CAN BE REACHED FROM THE A6075 AT KIRTON OR TUXFORD. THE PUB IS IN MAIN STREET. **PARKING:** AT THE OLD PLOUGH. LIMITED SPACE MAY ALSO BE FOUND BY THE CHURCH.

Egmanton is an attractive little village of about 200 souls on a junction of quiet roads, with a beck running beside the village street and a motte and bailey tucked away on Gaddick Hill, behind the church. The church itself, a beautiful building in the Anglo-Catholic tradition, was restored by John Comper at the end of the 19th century, at the expense of the Duke of Newcastle, and is dedicated to Our Lady of Egmanton. A local tradition maintains that, at some time away back in the Middle Ages, the Blessed Virgin appeared to a local woman in Ladywood, just over a mile away on the edge of the parish. The dedication to Our Lady was recorded as long ago as 1531, and the shrine was known as a place of pilgrimage right up to its destruction by 'reformers' at the time of the Reformation. With the restoration of the church, the shrine was also restored and regular pilgrimages have again been held since 1929, right up to the present day.

This walk follows quiet lanes, byways and field paths over the wooded arable country between Egmanton and Laxton. The paths are lightly used, but easily traceable, with no stiles to negotiate on the route of the walk.

The Old Plough Inn

The Old Plough is owned by Commer Inns and is a typical village hostelry where a long tradition of cheerful and friendly service is clearly being maintained. The inn was originally built as farm cottages but was converted to licensed premises in 1839. There is a full range of food on offer – bar snacks as well as full meals – and the 'Special Menu' includes such mouthwatering delicacies as giant Yorkshire pudding filled with sausage and mash, steak and kidney pie, lasagne verdi and chilli and rice.

The pub is open all day, every day; from 11 am to 11 pm on Monday to Saturday and between 12 noon and 10.30 pm on Sundays. Families are welcome, so are well-behaved dogs, and there is an outside drinking area. Telephone: 01777 872565.

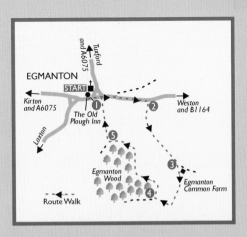

The Walk

① Starting from the pub, turn left along Main Street, then take the right fork (Weston Road) at the road junction. Follow the road away from the village for about ¹/₂ mile.

② Turn right onto a farm lane – waymarked by the guidepost opposite as a public bridleway. Coming here in late June, the writer found the wayside rich with the beautiful blue flowers of meadow cranesbill.

③ On the approach to Egmanton Common Farm, turn right over the concrete hard standing, making for a guidepost. Follow the edge of the field as directed, with the hedge on your left, turning right where the overhead wires cross. Continue to the end of this field, turning right again at the end and still following the hedgeside.

④ On reaching Egmanton Wood, turn right once more, following the perimeter of the wood. (If there is a growing crop, it may be easier – and perhaps excusable – to follow the 'tramlines' left by the farmer's tractor.) Over the next half mile or so, the line of the path (and the edge of the wood) bends left and right, without any barriers to progress. Towards the northern end of the wood, the landscape ahead opens out, with wide views to the north and round to Egmanton village.

PLACES OF INTEREST NEARBY

The village of **Laxton**, south of Egmanton, is the last place in England where the medieval open field system of agriculture still survives intact. The Court Leet meets here in the Dovecote Inn to administer the system, and there is a Visitor Centre, with its own car park adjacent to the inn.

Egmanton church

When a hedge does eventually intervene, pass through the gap (it may be a little tight!) and continue, still to the right of the wood. Bear right with the path, over the field, to reach a farm lane (Wood Lane).

⑤ Turn right and follow Wood Lane back to Weston Road. Turn left here for the village (and the Old Plough). Or, if you wish to visit the church, follow the guideposted route opposite, across the footbridge and over the field.

Nether Langwith
The Jug and Glass

| **MAP:** OS EXPLORER 28 (270) (GR 534705) | **WALK 23** | **DISTANCE:** $3^3/_4$ MILES |

DIRECTIONS TO START: NETHER LANGWITH LIES WEST OF THE A60 MANSFIELD-WORKSOP ROAD. APPROACHING FROM THE A614 (OLLERTON ROUNDABOUT) FOLLOW THE A616 NORTH-WEST TO CUCKNEY, THEN CONTINUE FOR 2 MILES ON THE A632. THE JUG AND GLASS IS SET BACK ON THE RIGHT. **PARKING:** IN THE JUG AND GLASS CAR PARK (PATRONS ONLY), OR ALONGSIDE THE ROAD FRONTING THE PUB.

It is called Nether Langwith to distinguish itself from the larger settlement of Langwith, just over the county boundary in Derbyshire, which developed on the shoulders of the mining industry. Nether Langwith itself has been largely unaffected by its close proximity to the collieries and has retained the pleasant atmosphere of a traditional country village. An area clearly influenced by its presence within Sherwood Forest and the Welbeck Abbey estate, the seeker after quiet recreation will find pleasant woodland here, and well-tended farmland, with a plentiful supply of quiet rural lanes and footpaths on which to stretch the legs.

The Jug and Glass

There can be few more perfect settings for a typical English country pub than that of the Jug and Glass which stands back from the road, overlooking the village green and the little River Poulter. A former coaching inn and one of Hardys and Hansons (Kimberley Brewery) houses, the earliest recorded licensee was here in 1787, although the building is almost certainly a great deal older, with possible connections going back to the days when the monks of Welbeck Abbey farmed the land. Families are welcome here (the facilities include a family room), and non-smoking areas are provided. And the outside drinking area is perfect!

Food is served daily from Monday to Saturday, between 11.30 am and 2.30 pm and in the evenings from 6 pm until 9 pm, and there is a splendid selection of seafood, chicken, grills, vegetarian dishes and traditional favourites, as well as a choice of snacks, salads and sandwiches. A traditional Sunday lunch is served from 12 noon until 2 pm.

The pub is open all day from Monday to Saturday; on Sunday the hours are 12 noon until 4 pm and 7 pm until 10.30 pm. Bed and breakfast is also available. Telephone: 01623 742283.

The Walk

① Cross the road and follow the facing lane, passing Brook House Farm and continuing ahead along the unmetalled way. Swing left with the lane through Boon Hills Wood.

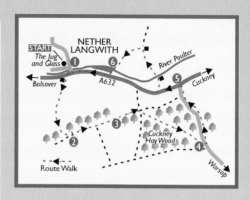

② On the next bend – a hairpin – cross the stile in front and continue along the intimate path on the edge of the wood. The way bends right and left, before leaving the wood against a long wooden seat (or a redundant stile?). As you emerge, keep straight forward, to the left of the facing hedge, crossing an open field, with the woodlands parallel on the left. At the end of the field, pass through the gap in the hedge and cross a farm lane.

③ Continue ahead via the footpath, just inside the wood, swinging right at a junction of paths. A little way on, break left onto a narrower way through the heart of Cuckney Hay Wood. Keep to the same general line through a confusion of crossing ways and the occasional wet patch (apart from which it is easy and delightful woodland walking all the way) to emerge onto an unclassified road in the south-east corner of the wood.

④ Turn left. Despite its lack of classification, this road is quite busy and has neither footway nor practicable verge, so keep well into the right, especially on right-hand bends.

Cuckney Hay Wood

⑤ Turn left again at the main (A632) road. Leave the road at the Goff's Restaurant entrance drive. Follow the drive past Mill House, continuing via the succeeding farm lane. Opposite Pasture Hill Farm, turn left through the gateway (or over the stile) and follow the left-hand hedge beneath the overhead wires. Part way up the field, cross a stile on the left, and cut across the corner of the next field to reach a second stile. Continue on the same line to the left-hand end of Langwith Lodge Lake.

⑥ Cross the stile at the foot of the lake, turning left and right with the fence and continuing via the footpath to the road. Emerge with great care, as the path exits directly onto the carriageway. Cross over to the footpath and turn right, following the road back to the Jug and Glass.

PLACES OF INTEREST NEARBY

Creswell Crags, Crags Road, Welbeck, near Worksop. The site spans the Nottinghamshire/ Derbyshire county boundary on the B6042, between the A616 and the A60. A picturesque setting of a limestone gorge with a lake, and caves; the home, 45,000 years ago, of Ice Age hunters. There is a Visitor Centre with computer interactives, audio-visual programmes and a gift shop. Admission to the site is free, but there is a charge for guided cave tours. Telephone: 01909 720378.

East Drayton
The Blue Bell

MAP: OS EXPLORER 271 (GR 777753)	**WALK 24**	DISTANCE: $3\frac{3}{4}$ MILES

DIRECTIONS TO START: VIA THE A57 (WORKSOP-LINCOLN) ROAD TO DARLTON, JUST EAST OF THE JUNCTION WITH THE A6075 FROM TUXFORD. FOLLOW THE UNCLASSIFIED LANE NORTH FROM DARLTON FOR ONE MILE, TURNING RIGHT AT THE CROSSROADS FOR THE BLUE BELL. **PARKING:** IN THE BLUE BELL CAR PARK (PATRONS ONLY) OR, TIDILY, ON NEIGHBOURING ROADSIDES.

East Drayton is a pleasant village of rather over 200 souls which, despite some modern building, still conveys an atmosphere of bygone days with its fine old church and traditional red brick and pantiled housing. Until the construction, in 1832, of the Dunham toll bridge over the Trent, the village stood on the through road to Laneham Ferry. Much more secluded today, it well deserves its designation as a conservation area. The 17th century architect Nicholas Hawksmoor, who worked with Christopher Wren and Vanburgh on many outstanding London buildings, was a son of East Drayton, having been raised on one of the local farms.

An unusual walk this, in that it involves a complete circuit of two massive fields – and very little else. This has distinct advantages, because the footpaths have been diverted around the perimeter of these fields, with wide grass tracks virtually all the way and with none of the problems presented by gates and stiles.

The Blue Bell

Families are welcome at the Blue Bell, a listed building where beamed ceilings and open coal fires accentuate the old world atmosphere. This is one of the Wolverhampton and Dudley Breweries' houses, open daily from noon until 2 pm (4 pm on Saturdays and Sundays) and in the evenings from 6 pm until 11 pm. Meals and bar snacks are served here, with a wide selection of home-cooked foods at reasonable prices. A special Early Bird selection is available between noon and 2 pm and from 6 to 8 pm; and specialities of the house include home-made shepherd's pie, steak and kidney pie, and gammon, egg and chips. Vegetarian meals are also available, and the selection of bar snacks includes sandwiches, chip butties and Blue Bell Burgers. There is a separate restaurant area, for which advance booking is advisable. Well-behaved dogs are welcome and there is an outside drinking area as well as a children's play area. Overnight accommodation can be provided. Telephone: 01777 248322.

The Walk

Note: Most of this route is ideally suited for use by wheelchair users. However, part of the section to the west of the Darlton road is over cultivated fields, with no suitable alternative rights of way available. For this reason, wheelchair users are advised to omit this section completely, and to follow Top Street and the Darlton road, turning left immediately before Green Acres to join the main route at

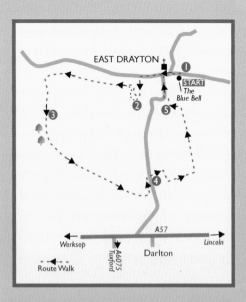

point 4. (Total adjusted distance $2\frac{1}{4}$ miles.)

① Leave the village via Church Lane, continuing past the houses and turning left into a broad green lane.

② At the top end of the lane turn right, crossing a footbridge. The right of way here follows the hedge right and left around two fields, before emerging onto a broad, green track and turning right. Turn left again with the track and, at the next turning, pass through a gap in the facing hedge and continue along the right-hand side of two more fields, turning left along

PLACES OF INTEREST NEARBY

Kingshaugh House, Lincoln Road, Darlton (on the A57, south of East Drayton). An ancient site dating back to Neolithic times, with evidence also found of Iron Age and Romano-British occupation. Visiting by appointment only; telephone: 01777 871870.

The walk follows a superb green track

the far end to cross a shallow ditch and rejoin the broad green way.

③ From here on, a right of way exists along the green track for the whole of its length. A superb track, it makes for easy strolling all the way, as it continues around the perimeter of this massive field, all the way to the Darlton road – where you turn left.

④ Pass Green Acres and turn right, again following a similar superb green way around the perimeter of one field; smaller, this one, than the previous prairie, yet still quite impressive. Continue around three sides of this field, finally turning right by a row of large barns.

⑤ Continue along an avenue of young trees, turning left at the end to reach the road (Top Street). Turn right now, back to the Blue Bell.

Church Laneham
The Ferry Boat Inn

MAP: OS EXPLORER 271 (GR 814767)   **WALK 25**   **DISTANCE:** 3½ MILES

DIRECTIONS TO START: VIA THE A57 (WORKSOP-LINCOLN) ROAD. TURN OFF NORTH (LANEHAM ROAD) ONE MILE WEST OF THE DUNHAM TOLL BRIDGE. FOLLOW LANEHAM VILLAGE STREET RIGHT THROUGH, CONTINUING ON TO CHURCH LANEHAM. **PARKING:** AT THE FERRY BOAT (PATRONS ONLY). SOME ROADSIDE PARKING SPACE MAY ALSO BE FOUND, SUBJECT TO SEASONAL RESTRICTIONS.

Church Laneham lies about half a mile to the east of the main village of Laneham. The principal building in this tiny riverside settlement is, needless to say, the beautiful parish church, a distinctive feature of which is the ancient Norman door, believed to be about nine hundred years old and one of the oldest in the country. The attractive half-timbered porch is equally interesting, though nothing like as venerable, having been constructed in the 20th century. The river is tidal here, but the ferry – like so many others up and down the Trent valley – is now consigned to history. This pleasant little stretch of river is still very popular with picnickers and strollers, particularly on balmy summer days.

The walk described here follows the banks of a pleasant little stream to Laneham village, from where we trace a circular route over the fields to the outskirts of Dunham on Trent and back. The close proximity (just over the river) of Lincolnshire clearly has an influence on local agricultural practice, some of the fields being of almost prairie dimensions!

The Ferry Boat Inn

The Ferry Boat is a truly traditional, early 18th century riverside country pub of a character rarely seen today. The setting and ambience are perfect and the service helpful and obliging. This is a free house serving, among others, Mansfield ales. The weekday opening hours (Monday to Friday) are from 12 noon until 4 pm and 7 pm (8 pm in winter) and 10.30 pm, with all day opening, from noon, on Saturdays and Sundays. Children are welcome, and there is a family room. Parties can be accommodated, with advance notice. And dogs are welcome, in the outside drinking areas only.

Meals and bar snacks are served daily from 12 noon until 2 pm in the week and 3 pm at the weekend. There is a wide range of traditional dishes and sweets on offer, and various sandwiches and baguettes for those of simpler taste, as well as a separate menu for the children. Traditional Sunday lunch is also available, for which advance booking is advised. Telephone: 01777 228350.

The Walk

Note: The total distance can be reduced a little by leaving the road at the first 'RUPP' sign – by the sluice gate – thus omitting the 'caravan site' section (and sacrificing a good view of the river).

① Follow the road north from the pub, passing the public toilets. There is a good view over the river here which, at this point, is quite impressive. Pass the entrance to the Manor House Caravan

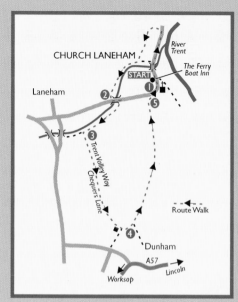

Park. Turn left at the next RUPP (Road Used as a Public Path) guidepost, following an unmade lane. Bend left with the track, which reverts to a lightly trodden green lane, sometimes wet underfoot. Continue ahead to join a streamside footpath, turning right.

② On reaching the road turn left. Cross the bridge and turn right over a stile, now following the top of the flood bank on the left side of the stream. Pass a footbridge (do not cross) and continue, now following the Trent Valley Way.

③ Turn left by the next stile (again, do not cross it), as directed by the footpath guidepost, descending to cross another stile and still following the Trent Valley Way. This path is not heavily used and may be overgrown at this point. Once over the stile there should be a clear path on the left of the dike (encroaching crops permitting!). At the end of one long field a farm track is joined, crossing the dike and

Church Laneham

now continuing on its right-hand side (Chequers Lane).

④ On the bend by Manor Farm, cross a stile on the left, following the waymarked route beside the hedge. In the next field, the waymarked route follows the right-hand hedge straight ahead and then sharp left. A more obvious way follows the farm track (but may, technically, be trespassing). Either way, ignore a footbridge on the right and continue to the top of the field, where a stile leads on into the next prairie. Keep to the left of the hedge all the way, with Cottam Power Station prominent ahead. After crossing a footbridge, the way continues as a green farm track, leading to the public road.

⑤ Turn right, back to Church Laneham and the Ferry Boat.

PLACES OF INTEREST NEARBY

Walks of Life Heritage Centre at 33, Lincoln Road, Tuxford (reached on the A6075 south-west of Church Laneham). Social history on wheels, with a fascinating collection of old trade handcarts. Telephone: 01777 870427.

Clarborough
The Gate Inn

DIRECTIONS TO START: THE VILLAGE OF CLARBOROUGH IS ON THE A620 (RETFORD TO GAINSBOROUGH) ROAD. LEAVE THE A620 ON THE BEND, AS FOR HAYTON, TURNING LEFT IMMEDIATELY ONTO SMEATH LANE AND CONTINUING OVER THE CANAL BRIDGE. THE GATE IS HERE, ON THE LEFT. **PARKING:** AT THE GATE INN (CAR PARK EXTENSION) (PATRONS ONLY); OR, WHERE SPACE AND SAFETY PERMIT, ALONGSIDE NEIGHBOURING ROADS.

Lying, as it does, on the main road close to Retford, and with good communications, Clarborough is today something of a dormitory village, with many of the inhabitants commuting to Rampton Hospital and the Trent Valley power stations. In recent years, the County Council has designated the village a growth area, which has led to a considerable increase in population. A lively village, there is a wide range of activities available here for all age groups and interests. And the added attractions of the Chesterfield Canal and a choice selection of public rights of way provide rest and relaxation for angler and stroller alike.

A pleasant circuit of the local ways takes us right round the village perimeter. First along quiet field paths running parallel to the main street; then onward to join and follow the towpath way back to our canalside 'watering hole'.

The Gate Inn

An attractive canalside free house providing first rate food and friendly service. Parts of the building pre-date the canal, going back to the 1700s, and the traditional atmosphere, displayed in the ancient beams and half-timbering, is complemented by the more recent purpose-built dining area, which overlooks the canal – as also does the outside drinking area.

Food is served daily, at lunchtime and in the evenings, full meals and bar snacks. Particular favourites include chicken, smoked bacon and mushroom pie, half a roast duck; and king-sized mixed grill. A selection of freshly made salads and sandwiches is available to order. Opening hours in the week are from 11.30 am until 2.30 pm and 5 pm to 11.30 pm; Sundays from 12 noon until 4 pm and 6 pm to 10.30 pm. Telephone: 01777 703397.

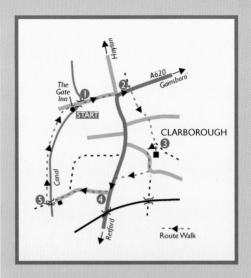

The Walk

① Cross the canal bridge and follow Smeath Lane. At the road junction turn right, and immediately left, now following the A620 uphill out of Clarborough, using the footway on the right.

② Leave the road via a waymarked footpath on the right, crossing a stile. Keep to the field boundary on your right, proceeding parallel to Clarborough Main Street and descending via a sunken way to join an unclassified road. Cross the road, bearing left a little as you do so, to resume the footpath way (by a 'No Dumping' sign) through a wooded area. Continue, again on the left of the hedge.

③ Turn right at a graveyard, descending between the church and the school building, to reach the road and turn left. Where the road bends left, keep ahead, joining the lane in front (The Baulk). Cross a stile on the right (no waymark) and follow the left-hand hedge down the field. Cross a concealed stile in the extreme corner and continue on the same line as before, passing to the left of a water trough to reach a farm gate and the road. Turn left.

④ Turn right at the next road junction (Bone Mill Lane). In passing, note Well House on your left. A spring beneath the house, known as St John's Well, was

PLACES OF INTEREST NEARBY

The Wetlands Waterfowl and Exotic Bird Park, Sutton-cum-Lound off the A638 north-west of Retford. Many species of wildfowl, birds of prey, owls, parrots, rheas, llamas, deer and farm animals, wild flowers and fungi, all in an attractive setting. Open daily, all year (except Christmas Day). Telephone: 01777 818099.

The lane past Bonemill Farm

celebrated, three hundred years ago, as a healing well. Continue to Bonemill Farm and over the canal bridge.

⑤ Descend the access path on your left to join the canal towpath. Pass under the bridge and continue back to the Gate Inn.

Carlton in Lindrick
The Blue Bell

MAP: OS EXPLORER 279 (GR 591844)   **WALK 27**   DISTANCE: 3³/₄ MILES

DIRECTIONS TO START: CARLTON IN LINDRICK IS SITUATED ON THE A60 ROAD, BETWEEN WORKSOP AND TICKHILL. THE BLUE BELL IS ON THE EASTERN SIDE OF THE MAIN ROAD. **PARKING:** AT THE BLUE BELL (PATRONS ONLY) OR ON-STREET, AWAY FROM THE MAIN ROAD.

Carlton in Lindrick stands astride the A60, with many of its finer features tucked away off the main road and out of sight of the casual passer-by. The tower of the parish church, on the quiet winding way through South Carlton, is largely of Saxon origin, and there is a good deal of herringbone masonry in the brickwork. Also of interest is the nearby Carlton Mill, with its cast-iron waterwheel which was supplemented by steam power in times of drought. The mill is now a museum, where the mill machinery can be seen, together with associated items, rural tools and so on. Carlton Cycles – which became an element of the Raleigh Company – began here as a cycle repair business founded by Mr Fred Hanstock. Local gardeners – Carlton was once known as 'The Rose Village' – developed the Carlton Daffodil.

This gentle stroll takes us along quiet field paths and lanes to Hodsock Priory, the site, in springtime, of a glorious display of snowdrops.

The Blue Bell

The Blue Bell, built about three centuries ago, retains much of the atmosphere of a traditional village inn. This is a free house, where you will find friendly service in congenial surroundings. Families are welcome here; dogs, too, in the attractive and secluded outside garden area. The pub is open all day, every day, and food is available – meals and bar snacks – from 12 noon until 9 pm on Monday to Saturday and between noon and 4 pm on Sundays. Main meals include an astonishing range of starters, followed by an equally impressive selection of steaks, grills, chicken, seafood and vegetarian dishes. Friday is speciality fish day, with haddock fresh in from Grimsby. Bar snacks include sandwiches, baguettes and beef-burgers. Telephone: 01909 730291.

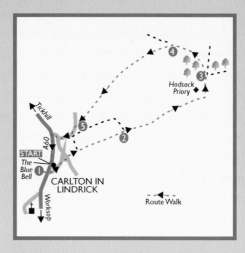

The Walk

① Turn left out of the pub, and left again by the Methodist chapel (Chapel Gate). Continue round by Low Street, bearing right at The Cross. At the junction with Greenway, turn left and immediately right, following an enclosed footpath out of the village. Ignore a side turning on the left, continuing straight ahead over an easy field path with good solid stiles.

② Emerging onto a farm lane, turn right, continuing ahead to Hodsock Priory. Not really a priory, it is nevertheless an imposing building with beautiful gardens. These are open to the public on occasion, especially in February, when the woods, in particular, host a glorious

display of snowdrops. Follow the access road round and past the Priory Farm Guest House.

③ On the bend by the Gatehouse entrance, leave the road, passing through a farm gate and following the waymarked route to the right of Horse Pasture Wood. Bear left at the end of the woods, through

Convolvulus

Hodsock Priory

a metal farm gate and onto a farm track.

④ On reaching a crossway, turn left. It will be noticed that there are paths here on either side of the hedge. The one on the left appears to be the more appropriate – but they both meet eventually, where the way passes through a gap by a gate, to enter a green lane. This graduates by degrees into a hard track leading to North Carlton.

⑤ The lane joins Woodhouse Lane – a metalled road – and, after bending right by Hodsock Lane, continues ahead to meet Greenway. Turn right here, and left at High Road, back to the Blue Bell.

PLACES OF INTEREST NEARBY

Langold Country Park, just off the A60 north of Carlton in Lindrick, has 400 acres of parkland and woods, ideal for gentle walks and picnics. There is a large lake, which is excellent for fishing, and which attracts a wide variety of wildlife. The park is open daily from dawn to dusk. Telephone enquiries to Bassetlaw District Council: 01909 475531.

North Wheatley
The Sun Inn

DIRECTIONS TO START: VIA THE A620 (RETFORD-GAINSBOROUGH) ROAD. LEAVE BY TURNING ON THE SOUTH SIDE OF DUAL CARRIAGEWAY, 2 MILES NORTH-EAST OF CLARBOROUGH. **PARKING:** AT THE SUN INN (PATRONS ONLY) OR ALONGSIDE THE ADJACENT OLD ROAD.

The twin villages of North and South Wheatley are virtually one today, though the church and the bulk of the community are contained within the northern boundaries. This is one of those blessed townships which, although in theory situated on a busy main road, have been immunised against the worst effects of passing traffic by the building of a bypass. A curious feature of North Wheatley is the 'Old Hall', a large brick-built 17th century building bearing the arms of the Cartwright family. The local economy, as might be supposed, is largely agricultural, much of the land being given over to sheep rearing and arable production. And Wheatley strawberries have also earned quite a reputation.

An easy-going walk with no stiles to negotiate begins with a road walk, calling for some care of passing traffic. Once clear of the main road, though, it is all quiet lanes and byways, with just one gentle climb, along a section of the Trent Valley Way.

The Sun Inn

The Sun shares the twin advantages of lying within the village of North Wheatley, convenient for the local trade, while being easily found, and reached, from the main A620 bypass. A fine and attractive free house with a roomy lounge, you will find a ready welcome here, and cheerful, courteous service. A large and comprehensive menu from which you may partake of starter, main course and dessert is balanced by a full range of bar snacks and light bites. Sunday lunches are served here, and there is a separate restaurant. The inn has all the usual facilities: a family room, children's play area, smoke-free zone and outside drinking area. And dogs are permitted, if well behaved.

Opening hours are from 11 am to 3 pm and 6.30 pm to 11 pm in the week (Monday to Friday), with all day opening at the weekend. Telephone: 01427 880210.

The Walk

Note: This route should be manageable with wheelchairs, although there is a certain amount of roadwork and some uneven ground.

① Follow the old road, which crosses the pub's frontage to join the west-bound main road, crossing over then to join the paved path. After about $1/2$ mile the path ends. This is a busy road, so keep well in to the right-hand verge for safety's sake. Continue for a further $1/2$ mile.

② Passing a house on your right you

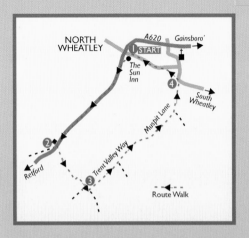

come to a farm gate carrying the legend 'Klondyke'. Cross the road here, taking the side turning to follow the lane for Clarborough Grange Farm. Negotiate a double bend and continue, passing a side turning, and entering Blue Stocking Lane.

③ A short distance further on, turn left (there is no waymark) following a clear field path to the right of the hedge and a pylon and following the line of the Trent Valley Way (Muspit Lane). The way climbs gently now for a while, after which the cooling towers of West Burton Power Station – one of several such strewn up and down the Trent Valley – come into view ahead, to the right. Continue ahead

PLACES OF INTEREST NEARBY

Sundown Kiddies' Adventureland (Pets Garden), Treswell Road, Rampton. Adventure for the children (ideal for under-10s) with Smugglers' Cove, Western Street, Fantasy Castle and much more. Reached via Treswell to the south-east of North Wheatley, or from the A57, 3 miles from the Dunham on Trent crossroads. Telephone: 01777 248274.

A field path at North Wheatley

along a clear unmade lane to South Wheatley.

④ At a road junction turn left. You can follow the road round, turning left at the next junction, to reach the Sun Inn. But a pleasanter – and slightly shorter – way (but not for wheelchairs) goes via a field-path to the left of the 'School' sign, thus cutting a corner.

Scaftworth
The King William

MAP: OS EXPLORER 279 (GR 664918)   WALK 29   DISTANCE: 3½ MILES

DIRECTIONS TO START: SCAFTWORTH LIES OFF THE A631 (SOUTH SIDE) JUST OVER A MILE SOUTH-EAST OF BAWTRY. THE KING WILLIAM IS SITUATED ALONGSIDE THE VILLAGE'S SINGLE LOOP ROAD. **PARKING:** AT THE KING WILLIAM (PATRONS ONLY) OR, TIDILY, ALONGSIDE VILLAGE STREET. LAY-BYS ARE ALSO AVAILABLE ON EITHER SIDE OF THE A631.

Scaftworth is so small and secluded that I have been unable to find any mention of it in my collection of Nottinghamshire guidebooks. A privately owned village, I am informed, and consisting of little more than a hall, a farm, the pub and a handful of traditional cottages, this charming hamlet nestles in a pretty rural spot alongside the River Idle. The sort of blessed plot that must be bypassed each year by many thousands of travellers along the adjacent busy Gainsborough road, all totally unaware of its existence. A place which nobody visits except for a reason.

A short journey by quiet country tracks brings us to Barrow Hills, where we stroll through delightful mixed woodland high above the main road in a loop of the Idle. The return journey follows lower ground along peaceful farm roads and green lanes.

The King William

A 'Les Routières' listed free house, the King William is run as a low-key operation with the aim of maintaining the atmosphere of a traditional country pub. The discerning visitor will find here all the facilities he is likely to demand: a family room and children's play area, a large and attractive riverside garden, good ales and food – and perfect rural peace.

Although the outside board suggests that the pub does not open at lunchtime between Monday and Thursday, we are told there is some flexibility, so a telephone call may clarify the position. Lunchtime opening from Friday to Sunday is between 12 noon and 3 pm. Evening opening on Monday to Saturday is from 6.30 pm to 11 pm and on Sunday from 7 pm until 10.30 pm. Food is available whenever the pub is open, last orders being taken at 2.30 pm and 9.00 pm. Home-made soups, pâtés and pies are a speciality, as also are pints of prawns and prime English steaks. The menu varies weekly. Some overnight accommodation can be provided too. Telephone: 01302 710292.

Gastronomes will no doubt be thrilled to know that this is the home of the English Snail Company, with snails always available on the menu (and, alive, to take away – ugh!). Subject to reasonable notice (and an optional contribution to village fund-raising), a visit can be arranged to the snail farm ...

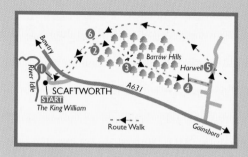

The Walk

① Turn left from the pub; then right again into a green byway, continuing to reach the A631. Cross the dual carriageway and continue ahead, along Theaker Lane.

② About ½ mile on, turn right and follow the footpath to the left of a tall oak tree and the succeeding hedgerow, ascending towards the hilltop wood (Barrow Hills). When alongside the wood, branch off right onto a side path, climbing steeply into the heart of the wood. Remain with the footpath all the way, through beautiful mature broadleaved woodland.

③ On the hilltop, continue beside successive blocks of conifers (still with broadleaves on your right). As you approach the eastern end of the woods bear right and descend via a sandy pathway to reach the exit gate.

④ Follow the lane (Pinfold Lane) down to the hamlet of Harwell and turn left. Continue to the next turning on the left –

PLACES OF INTEREST NEARBY
Mattersey Priory, Mattersey (off the A631, south of Everton). Remains of a small Gilbertine monastery; open at any reasonable time, admission free.

Delightful woodland at Barrow Hills

Pasture Lane (there is a guidepost at the junction).

⑤ Follow Pasture Lane, a good, wide farm lane. At the entrance to Pasture Farm, this lane swings right. Continue straight forward here, along a lesser track, with Barrow Hills on your left. This track reverts to a green lane and becomes Theaker Lane.

⑥ The outward route is rejoined by the tall oak – continue ahead from here, back to the dual carriageway and Scaftworth.

Misterton
The Packet Inn

MAP: OS EXPLORER 280 (GR 775947)   **WALK 30**   **DISTANCE:** 2½ MILES

DIRECTIONS TO START: FROM BECKINGHAM (ON THE A631 BETWEEN BAWTRY AND GAINSBOROUGH) FOLLOW THE A161, PASSING THROUGH WALKERINGHAM. AT MISTERTON, IMMEDIATELY AFTER PASSING BENEATH THE RAILWAY BRIDGE, TURN RIGHT ALONG STATION ROAD. THE PACKET INN IS ON THE RIGHT, OVER THE CANAL BRIDGE. **PARKING:** BONA FIDE PATRONS MAY LEAVE THEIR VEHICLES IN THE SPACIOUS PACKET INN PARKING AREA. NON-PATRONS ARE ADVISED, IF IN DOUBT, TO PARK TIDILY ON STATION ROAD

Misterton extends for about a mile along the A161 road, the oldest part being at the western end, around the B1403 road junction. We are told that King Charles I appointed a Dutch engineer, Sir Cornelius Vermuyden, to drain the marshes which now constitute the Isle of Axholme and the quality of the resulting arable land brought work, and a flourishing economy, to the district. The arrival of the Chesterfield Canal in the late 18th century brought further prosperity, the local clay excavated in the works proving ideal for brick-making. Several brickworks were opened here, one appropriate end use of the bricks being the construction of canal locks and bridges. A busy village today, the local economy embraces light and heavy industry, as well as agriculture.

This short walk begins with a circuit of the arable fields to the north of the village, leading to a pleasant stroll through the old village, and continuing with a saunter along the Chesterfield Canal, back to the Packet Inn.